**MORE REMARKABLE, TRUE STORIES
OF ONE OF AUSTRALIA'S GREAT COPS**

TOPCOP 2
ON THE BEAT

Chief Inspector Gary Raymond APM, OAM (Rtd)
BY DAVID R. NICHOLAS

Ark House Press
PO Box 1722, Port Orchard, WA 98366 USA
PO Box 1321, Mona Vale NSW 1660 Australia
PO Box 318 334, West Harbour, Auckland 0661 New Zealand
arkhousepress.com

Ark House Press, a division of Initiate Media.

All rights reserved. No part of this publication may be reproduced, stored in a retrieval system or transmitted in any form or by any means electronic, mechanical, photocopying, recording or otherwise without the prior written permission of the publisher.

© Ark House Press

ISBN: 9780992345280 (pbk.)

Cataloguing in Publication Data:
Title: Top Cop 2 On the Beat
ISBN: 9780992345280 (pbk.)
Subjects: Spiritual /Biography
Other Authors/Contributors: Nicholas, David

Cover design and layout by initiateagency.com

This book is dedicated to Elisabeth Elliot wife of Jim Elliot the missionary martyred in Ecuador. Years ago Elisabeth told me, "Tell it simply, tell it straight and see that it is true." This I have done to the best of my ability.

CONTENTS

Chapter One: Thieves Galore   7
- Weighed Down
- The Zirconia Crook
- The Balaclava Thief

Chapter Two: Weird Ways   17
- Protected by Prostitutes
- No Thanks, I'm Okay
- The Gutter Drunk
- Lightning Strikes the Force
- Taxi Driver in Attack Mode
- The Under the Bed Dad
- The Persons of Interest Tree
- King Hit Trapped by a Crusher
- Walking On Broken Glass
- Body In Drain
- Detective Discovers Truth Pays

Chapter Three: Tangled Ways   49
- Part One: Shockwaves
- Part Two: Coming to Terms
- Part Three: Power to Forgive

Chapter Four: Time For Tears   79
- Wheelchair Incident
- Dad Suicides
- Landside at Thredbo
- A Detective Cries
- A Murdered Baby
- Too Young to Die

Chapter Five: **Views From the Beat**   103
- On Criminals
- The Justice System
- The Human Touch
- View from the Hearse
- Vanishing Samaritans
- The Police Force

Chapter Six: **Strange Ways**   123
- Muddled Sexes
- Strip Search on Road
- A Bike that Slides
- Skippy's Wooden Leg
- The Witches Cove
- Man in Cell with Shaved Head
- Woman Prostitute on Highway
- Unconscious Truckie Prostitute
- The Razor Gang
- On Not Being Camera Shy
- The Man with the Iron Bar
- Trapped by Lollies
- A Dash with a Splash
- Grass Trap Door Dealers

Chapter Seven: **Raymond on Policing**   149
- A Christian in the Police Force
- Traps in Policing
- 'P' Plate Drivers
- Individuals and Speed
- An Empty Park
- A Word On Victims
- Capital Punishment

Chapter Eight: Red For Danger — 157
- Fire at Luna Park
- Bomb at the Hilton Hotel
- The Scar-Faced Kidnapper
- Danger in Court
- Asian Drug Dealers
- It's all in the Understanding
- Gun out of Window
- A French Stabber
- Drop the Gun

Chapter Nine: A Touch of Humour — 181
- A Truck Duck
- Abseiling to Inspector
- On Going Through the Roof
- The Black Plastic Caper
- Ladder to a Toilet

Chapter Ten: A Present Help — 191
- A Nephew Rescued
- Dragging Girl off Rail Tracks
- The Roof Wrestle
- On Taking the Heat
- Glass Crate Rescue
- A Sad Arrest
- Wrap Up

A Christian Policeman's Prayer — 201

Appendix: Suicide Awareness — 203

CHAPTER ONE

THIEVES GALORE

"We hang the petty thieves and appoint the
great ones to public office." *Aesop*

Whilst in Police Rescue Gary Raymond was called to a large warehouse in Alexandria, a Sydney suburb, in the early hours of the morning. It was a dark night with good weather. Three men in their mid twenties had broken into the factory via the tin roof. Two were quickly arrested by the police who had attended the scene after a call from security officers. The offenders were securely placed into the rear of a caged police van and, as usual, they weren't talking. The security officers said there'd been three thieves. The search for the third went ahead without success. Police knew the scene was surrounded, with no escape for the thief. They anticipated he may have climbed back up onto the factory's roof to escape detection. Gary and the late Sergeant Joe Beecroft arrived and as he gazed around, Gary saw a hole in the tin roof. Along with his Sergeant, Gary clambered up through the hole, presuming the missing thief had gone up to the roof. Once on the roof Gary and Joe searched around for the offender. Not a trace of him could be seen. As the two police searched the roof area, Joe Beecroft stepped on a sheet of roofing tin lying between two folds in the 'v' shaped roof. There was a deep metallic crunch followed by a very loud yell. Not a yell; it was more a high pitched shriek. As Joe's heavy police boot came down onto the iron, he wondered what he'd done after receiving an enormous fright. Gary jumped with shock. Without realising it, underneath the tin there was a person. The missing offender was hiding on his back under the sheet which he had used as a cover to avoid being seen at the bottom of the roof's 'v' section. Joe startled, jumped off the sheet and lifted it up to revel his catch. This caused Gary to roar with laughter as he searched and handcuffed the 'battered' offender who looked like he had just stepped out of the ring after a boxing match. The flexible sheet and the Sergeant's weight combined to give the offender a flattened, bloodied and bruised nose! The thief however was not amused. He didn't see the funny side of the event. He had a bruise or two to prove the result of his injury. This all goes to prove that often in trying to escape the long arm of the law, offenders can find themselves in a far worse position. In this case, hiding from police under a sheet of metal was certainly not a good idea nor the smartest thing to do. The boys in blue (white overalls for rescue) were a good match for this stealth offender. One could only hope he learnt from the error of his ways. Gary adds, "Maybe they should manufacture sheet tin with a 'nose shaped' indentation to save offenders, who hide under them, from suffering such a painful injury. "It's all about risk management," Gary said, sarcastically while laughing.

The Zirconia Crook
A doctor from Singapore was practising in Australia. He came to see Gary at the Blacktown Police Station to complain about a fraud offence committed against him. The complaint was about a male person who'd sold the doctor a whole lot of diamonds for thousands of dollars. After the sale and exchange of cash, the doctor took them to a jeweller for a valuation, which was required for insurance purposes. The jeweller only had to look at the diamonds once and said carefully, "I've got bad news for you doctor. These gems are not diamonds, they are cubic zirconia." The doctor nearly fainted and looked like he needed a doctor

himself. Not what the doctor had in mind when he parted with his money for the 'precious gems'. He had been ripped off in a big way by a huge scam.

Cubic zirconia is the cubic crystalline form of zirconium dioxide ($ZrO2$). The synthesized material is hard, optically flawless and usually colourless, but may be made in a variety of different colours. It can often be mistaken for diamonds to the untrained eye. Because of its low cost, durability and close visual likeness to diamond, synthetic cubic zirconia has remained the most important competitor for diamonds since commercial production began in 1976. These were not what the doctor had ordered.

Gary Raymond made enquiries and soon discovered there were others who had been ripped off. The amount involved was around $100,000. Gary also discovered the 'zirconia crook' had bought a property on the outskirts of Kempsey, New South Wales with his spoils. Gary and his detective partner flew to Kempsey on a regional airline and then borrowed a car from the local police station. They went to a property, executed a Search Warrant and arrested the offender. They found a large number of cubic zirconia, bank records and other documents to prove the offence. They took the offender and exhibits to the Kempsey Police Station. Interviews, charges and paperwork were completed.

That evening Gary and his mate went to the Kempsey Airport and boarded a twin engine propeller powered aeroplane back home to Sydney. There were nine or ten people on board and three crew. The plane took off shortly after dark. Just after takeoff, there was a loud noise followed by a catastrophic failure on the left engine of the aircraft. It suddenly compromised the plane's control systems and forward speed. The pilot and co-pilot struggled to guide the plane at first. They immediately put the nose down to keep airspeed, steadily turned and headed back to the airport. At one stage the plane flew above the treetops near Kempsey. They could see the plane's control panel was lit up like a Christmas tree with red and other coloured lights. Emergency alarm noises pierced the cockpit. Some were bipping and some were buzzing. They could hear the pilot talking on the radio to a control tower somewhere. At this time the plane was flying close to the ground. The pilot and co-pilot struggled as they tried to stop the plane from stalling. The pilot desperately tried to work the switch which would turn the Kempsey runway lights back on. The runway marker lights had been switched off after the plane left the runway. It was the last plane to leave for the night. From the plane's windows they could all see the lights of Kempsey Central Business District getting closer and closer. At this time, the passengers were truly scared and some were saying things like, "Oh my God, I don't want to die". "What in the hell's happening"? Some were greatly distressed, some were gasping, others were crying and shaking. Everyone's eyes were wide open watching the emergency unfold and contemplating their future, including Gary.

Gary reflecting said, "It's strange, but I was more concerned about the other people than myself. I wondered whether they were ready to die by knowing Jesus personally. I didn't want to die but knew I was ready because of what Christ did for me on the cross. I knew salvation was a gift and I couldn't earn it. Being an aviation enthusiast and former glider pilot, I was carefully watching the aircraft's behaviour, at the same time watching the gauges on the instrument panel. What were the gauges telling me? Were we going to land or crash? The only thing that really worried me was fire. I didn't know whether the engine failure included a fire or if our hard landing would cause a fire. I guessed the plane was full of fuel to get to Sydney. In the back of my mind I said to God, "Please if I am to die now, let me die in the crash impact, not be burnt to death". In the Ambulance Service and Police Rescue Squad, I had attended a large number of people seriously burnt or burnt to death and it wasn't pretty. I wondered what it would be like to end up that way. My thoughts went back to the plane's condition and what the pilot and co-pilot were doing. I became very alert and noticed every move, every sight, every sound and every feeling of my emotions. Many people say they saw their life go before them at such times as this, I didn't. I was glued in the present tense. My past didn't mean anything; it was surviving the present crisis that filled my mind. I stayed calm and had made up my mind I had no control whatsoever over what was happening to me. Don't get me wrong, I still hoped and prayed we would land safely on one engine. I thought, "Will the damaged engine break off? What if the plane broke up after the damaged engine broke off? I was also contemplating what brace position I would adopt for impact."

Gary's detective partner appeared calm but anxiously said, "What are we going to do?" Gary said, "Just pray mate and ask Jesus to forgive your sin and give Him your life right now. God will listen to that prayer and if we die, you'll be with Him and me for eternity."

At this time, the plane was making an approach back into Kempsey airfield but the pilot was still struggling to hold the plane steady on a straight line. The flight attendant told everybody to take up the brace crash position. Gary left his head up as he wanted to see what was happening on the plane's approach to the airfield. Not like Gary to miss a trick. He thought he would put his head down at the last minute; no, the last second, which he did. The plane then landed very heavily on the runway, which had no guiding lights. Gary quickly put his head back up to see where the plane was going to end up. Only one engine was reverse thrusting and the pilots were 'standing' on the foot pedal brakes, not only to stop it, but keep it in a straight line. The plane came to a steady stop on the grass verge beside the runway. It had actually run slightly off the runway. "No worries, at least we were back on planet earth in one piece, thank you God," Gary confidently told me.

Gary said they all left the plane in a hurry and ran away in case the plane caught fire and exploded. Gary said he and his mate were helping the passengers down the steps. They then ran down the steps themselves and ran away from the plane. At a safe distance they stopped, looked back and discovered the plane was intact with no smoke or fire. It was then they heard the sirens as the fire, ambulance and rescue teams responding from outside the airport. The pilot asked everyone to walk to the terminal. Each had a look of relief on their face. Gary's detective mate, with relief in his voice, said with a grin, "I don't really believe in God you know." Gary sarcastically said, "Well, you nearly met Him today, whether you believe He exists or not!" After that every time Gary saw that particular detective Gary would ask, "Do you believe in God yet?" "Not yet but I'm sure I will one day," was his reply. Gary really thought he'd die that day. He thought that if he did die, at least it would have been sudden and quick. Gary told me it's an amazing feeling to be faced with your own death evrn though we face death every day from many causes. Disease, accident, foul play, self inflicted or other causes may suddenly or slowly 'take us out'. We don't dwell on it, but we have to be ready, just in case.

The crew and passengers walked across to the terminal which after being shut for the night became a flurry of activity. Airline ground crew were arranging alternative fights for the passengers. One middle aged businessman yelled a tirade of abuse. He told staff where they could 'stick' their aeroplanes and he was going to hire a car at their expense and drive back to Sydney. Gary thought that he would still be safer travelling by air, despite the recent drama, than driving along the Pacific Highway at night all the way to Sydney. Gary commented to me, "At least in the air you don't have speeding semi-trailers, sleepy car drivers or wandering kangaroos!"

Some other passengers decided to stay in Kempsey until the next day. However, Gary and his detective partner agreed to go by bus to Port Macquarie and get another plane to Sydney that same night. Whilst waiting, they went to a nearby hotel where they had a conversation with the pilot and co-pilot. Both pilots expressed relief that they had brought the plane back safely and that it was a 'close call' to lose an engine so soon after taking off. They had completed lots of training for such an emergency but it was still confronting to happen in a real time and place out of the simulator. They were both confident individuals. Gary joined them in expressing relief they had done such a good job. Gary laughed and told me, "At least we had one engine left. When I flew gliders, we had none all the time!"

The zirconia crook was given a gaol sentence for fraud and theft. Compensation was sought for the doctor but the criminal had no recoverable money.

Fakes may look attractive and real, but really they remain imitations. Jesus said, "I am the Way, the Truth and the Life. No one comes to the Father except by Me." (John 14:6) There is no other way to God other than through Christ. Just like the doctor was deceived with zirconias purporting to be diamonds, we can be deceived by fakes, and in the end, people lose not money, but eternal life with Christ. Jesus is the real Saviour and his love is more valuable than all the diamonds of earth. As George Beverly Shea used to sing, "I'd rather have Jesus than silver or gold".

The 'Balaclavaless' Thief
The owner of a local service station in Blacktown employed a new console operator. The owner gave him general instructions as to the running of petrol and product sales in the business. He then told him that if someone ever comes in with a weapon and demands money, give them all the money. Do not risk your life for money, no matter how much. During his training, the operator was shown where everything was stored, including the cash for the till which was hidden in various places throughout the premises.

Unfortunately about three months later, a man suddenly entered the service station wearing a balaclava, overalls and gloves. He was armed with a hand gun. He yelled loudly, "Give me all the money or I'll blow your brains out." The operator immediately immersed into terror and scooped the money out of the cash register. He then went to the drawer underneath and handed over the hidden money from there. The operator then went to a 'hidey-hole' in a cigarette cupboard nearby and gave the robber that money. There was some money hidden behind some lollies as well. This was also handed over. The giving over of money did not stop there, for there were some more coins in bags hidden in the back of a refrigerator and the operator gave this money to the crook as well. He did all this because the boss had said, "If a robber comes in and asks for money, give him all the money!" The operator sure carried out his boss's instructions, to the letter! He gave the offender every coin and notes known to be everywhere on the premises.

By this time, the robber was having trouble containing all the money he had been given. He had limited pockets in his overalls. Being greedy and overjoyed at his quick wealth, without thinking, he took off his balaclava, put the money in it and wrapped it up to make a bag type holder for all the money. What a windfall; more than he could ever have imagined. He then told the operator to lie on the ground and not to move. The robber left on foot with pockets and a balaclava full of cash. When safe to do so, the operator pushed the silent hold-up alarm button and police arrived. Detectives were then called for.

When he arrived at the service station, Gary and his detective mate talked to the operator who gave them a description of the offender.

He said, "I gave him all, the money."

He told the two detectives how he gave out the money from the various hidey-holes.

Gary asked, "Why did you give him the money from all the hidey-holes?"

"Because the boss told me to," he replied innocently.

Gary shrugged his shoulders, nodded and thought, "I can understand that."

THIEVES GALORE

Gary looked at the closed circuit TV footage in the petrol station office and noticed, much to his delight, the robber who took off his balaclava to carry more cash was a local offender who Gary knew well from previous arrests for other types of crimes. With no balaclava to hide his face, identification was very easy.

Gary said, "It was what we police call, 'a walk up start'."

The Scientific Section, as it was known then, attended to process the crime scene.

The detectives went to the man's house, which was not far away. They snuck up the side of the house and looked through the suspect's lounge room window. Gary saw the man sitting at a coffee table with a big cheesy grin. All the stolen money, both notes and coins was spread out on the table in its denominations. There was a gun on the floor. At a predetermined time, Gary's partner smashed the window with his police revolver and pointed it at the robber demanding he surrender. Gary too, armed with his police revolver broke down the front door, ran down the hallway to the lounge room and secured the offender's gun, at gun point. The offender was arrested and handcuffed. The grin turned into a terrified look on the offender's face. All the dreams of drugs, booze, women and holidays shattered. Again, the Scientific Section attended the second crime scene in the house.

Later, the robber asked Gary, "How did you know it was me, Mr. Raymond?" Gary answered slowly and sarcastically, "Well, you are a star mate. We saw you front and centre on the CCTV. You'd make an accomplished screen actor except you forgot your make-up. Remember, you took off your balaclava and filled it with money?" "Oh no," said the robber, hitting himself on the forehead for being so stupid. The man's love for money made him forget his disguise in the 'excitement' of the moment. Gary observed how greed can cause us to do things that destroy us. The result of this escapade? The service station robber got 7 years jail for that and other robberies. "He counted the money, but didn't count the cost," Gary wisely commented.

CHAPTER TWO

WEIRD WAYS

"I'm one of those regular weird people." *Janis Joplin (Singer)*

Protected by Prostitutes
A mother of seven children was attending church where Gary and his wife Michelle were trying to care and help her. One night while she was out, her 16 year old and 9 year old daughters wandered away from home looking for adventure.

The two went to King's Cross (the Cross) a place in Sydney known for the darker side of life. It's full of vice, prostitution, drugs and violence. They walked around enjoying the sights and sounds of an area where they had heard about but had never been before. All was well until the 9 year old became separated from her sister. The 16 year old panicked, went to a phone booth and phoned her mother. In a raging panic, the mother rang Gary to say her young daughter had disappeared in Kings Cross. Gary immediately rang the Police Communications Centre and they put out an all points alert to all police in the area. The 16 year old was told to go to Kings Cross Railway Station and stay there at the ticket barrier and wait for the police. Gary rang another Christian police officer and said, "We have a drama on our hands. Can you come and help me look for a missing 9 year old girl from our church in the Cross?"

Gary and his mate spoke to on-duty police. They formulated a search plan. The two started their search. They decided to do a search of all the pubs, nightclubs and strip joints in Kings Cross. Gary and his mate spoke to all the taxi drivers, security bouncers, bikers and drug dealers along the main street and asked them to let him know if they saw the missing girl. Gary and his mate started to search for the girl with a real sense of urgency. As the two off-duty police officers walked around, they talked to two prostitutes. They asked them to 'spread the word' around the brothels in the Cross and keep a lookout for the girl.

Gary told me, "You could see the panicked look on the prostitute's faces when I mentioned it was a 9 year old girl missing. The prostitutes used swear words in telling Gary they'd better find her quickly as what could happen to her in the Cross was too awful to even mention. The place was full of paedophiles, deviates and organised crime figures. Some of them would love to find a young girl to exploit for gratification, photographs, money or more.

"We were getting increasingly worried as time marched on," gary commented. The longer it took, the greater the danger. The tension in the air was palpable. There was also a risk she may be taken away from the Kings Cross precinct in a motor vehicle either willingly or forcefully, which added to our deep concerns."

Gary and his mate had conducted exhaustive searches and enquiries without result. Police on duty were also frantically looking and using all their 'street' connections and police informants to find the girl. General Duty, Drug Squad, Detectives, Highway Patrol and many police from adjoining areas joined in. Gary told everyone that he and his mate would go to McDonalds and make it a sort of 'temporary field headquarters' for the search. If the street people heard anything, they would ring the police immediately and then tell Gary at McDonalds as well. Gary remembered that many times in dire situations, he had advised people to pray about their circumstances. Praying is talking to God and letting Him talk to us. Now was the time for Gary to 'practise what he preached.' Gary and his mate bowed their heads, closed their eyes, sincerely prayed and asked God to bring the 9 year old girl safe and well to them at McDonald's.

An hour or so later, two female prostitutes entered McDonald's. One said to Gary, "Are you Detective Sergeant Gary Raymond?"

Gary showed his ID and replied anxiously, "Yes. What news do you have?"

They told Gary they knew where the girl was and that she was unharmed. They carefully explained that two of their prostitute colleagues had found the girl wandering the streets upset and lost. They knew she didn't 'belong' there and was in grave danger. They smuggled her into a brothel and hid her under a bed, in an unused room, to make sure no pimps would get hold of her. They kept her there until they found out the location of her parents. Gary and his mate stood up and wanted to go immediately and get the little girl. They were told "no", for the girls didn't want the police to know the location of their newly acquired brothel. They said they would get the girl straight away and bring her back to McDonald's. They left.

Gary was anxious and wondered whether he should covertly follow them. A doubt entered his mind. Could he trust them? They were after all part of the 'get what you can' street culture, making money for their drugs in any way possible. He thought that they would not have come to report the missing girl if they had other devious plans, so Gary settled down his thoughts and trusted God.

Triumphantly a short time later, they returned with the girl who was in tears. The first thing Gary asked was, "Are you alright?"

She replied with a dripping nose, "Yes Mr Raymond, I just got lost and was scared."

She was in fact, unharmed.

When questioned further, she said, "I got lost and couldn't find my sister. These two ladies took me and hid me under their bed. They were kind and helped me. I'm sorry I've been naughty, running away from home. Is mummy mad?"

Gary replied, "Yes, but I'm sure she'll be so glad we found you. Just settle down, it's okay." She was hungry, so Gary bought her a meal. The parents expected the police to find their daughter, but it was in fact prostitutes who found her and kept her safe.

As Gary and his mate had coffee with the two prostitutes at McDonald's, Gary said, "Ladies, I want you to know we are both Christian police officers. We prayed that God would find the girl. Do you ladies realise that God has used you both tonight to find the girl and bring her back safely?"

One of the women, shaking her head in disbelief, said, "God wouldn't use me. I'm a mole, a slut, you know. He probably hates my guts and is going to see me burn in hell."

Gary gently reinforced what he had said. "Look ladies, God has used you both. You both need to know that God forgave us all when Jesus died on the cross. He took the punishment from God that we all deserved after committing all of our sin. This sin is both now and in the future. He loves you and is waiting for you to come to Him and give up this dead-end lifestyle. One day we're all going to stand before Jesus. An adulterous woman once stood before Jesus and He said, "Neither do I condemn you, go and sin no more." (John 8:11) God will forgive you ladies if you believe in Him."

Gary bowed his head and prayed sincerely with the two ladies. After the prayer, the other woman said, "I can't pray, I'm addicted to heroin and I'm thirty years of age." Gary said, "You can be free of all of this mess if you just surrender to Jesus."

Gary said assertively but gently, "God trusted you enough to put this lost little girl in your hands tonight. Now put yourself in God's hands and trust Him for the rest of your life, starting tonight."

At this stage, both women had tears in their eyes. They thanked Gary and his mate very much for allowing them to help. Gary shook hands with them and the 'ladies of the night' disappeared into 'the night'. The two young girls were reunited with their desperately worried mother with lessons well learnt.

Gary said to me, "I wonder what became of those two prostitutes? I guess time, or should I say eternity will tell." Gary further stated, "I feel so deeply sad when I see people wreck their life with sin, crime, greed, lust, alcohol, drugs and everything else that harms them when they make bad choices. I've seen people from good and bad backgrounds make destructive choices. No matter what your upbringing, at the end of the day you personally make the choices. Even if your 'choice capacity' has been diminished for any reason, you still have enough God given conscience to make the right choices. God made sure of that when He created us. One bad choice leads to many more if the bad choices are not arrested in their tracks. Some people do a 'u' turn and recover; others just don't care anymore. It's all about them and them only. We should always reinforce to people the advantages of making good choices and not ever compromise by playing around with harmful behaviours."

No Thanks, I'm Okay
Gary was performing a shift from the Police Rescue Squad on one of the first Police helicopters. The first chopper was leased to the Police Force long before they purchased their own. It was hangered at Sydney Kingsford Smith Airport. A call came in that a volunteer lifesaver was being swept out to sea off Bondi Beach. Gary and his crew were in disbelief. A lifesaver in trouble? They're the ones that rescue us from the surf. They raced to the helicopter. The crew consisted of a pilot, observer, winch operator and rescuer. They were soon in the air and gained urgent clearance from Air Traffic Control to proceed. On the beach at Bondi, people indicated by waving their arms where the man was roughly located. He was at the southern end of the beach. Gary and his crew desperately searched for the man as every second, no every millisecond, counts when you're drowning. Gary's chopper did a grid search in sections of the ocean without success.

They flew further out to sea away from the 'shore' riptides to the ocean's currents. Gary suddenly spotted the lifesaver through his binoculars and informed the pilot. The pilot brought the helicopter down close to the water and hovered near the man who was swimming along calmly. Gary jumped from the helicopter's skid with a special helicopter rescue harness for the man. Gary was wearing a harness and life jacket himself. This harness is designed to hook onto the patient's harness for the winch lift into the chopper. Prior to the fitting of the winch, rescues were done with a rope slung on the cargo hook underneath the centre of the chopper or from the door between the skid and fuselage.

The ocean was in a metre swell with no white water. That meant Gary and the man were bopping up a metre and down a metre. Not an easy environment to work in. The rotor noise and water surface turbulence caused by the rotor downwash also made it difficult to communicate with the lifesaver. Gary swam alongside the man.

Surprisingly, the lifesaver yelled, "What are you doing here? I don't need you. I'm a lifesaver. I can manage. I'm trained for this."

Gary looked at the metre high waves and felt the strong ocean current and straight away doubted the man's judgement. The lifesaver further stated, "I'm swimming with the current and I'll get out just south of here."

Gary yelled sarcastically, "Mate from the chopper's view of the current, you'll end up in New Zealand, not back at the coast. You're going the wrong way mate and you'll not get out of this. Just put this harness on and we'll lift you up into the chopper and take you back to the beach."

He yelled, "No way. I will be fine. I'm a lifesaver. Leave me alone. Don't embarrass me."

Gary couldn't believe the lifesaver was refusing rescue assistance given his predicament. He wasn't being caught in a shoreline rip; it was the Tasman Sea current! Again, Gary gave him a last chance to be rescued. He angrily and aggressively refused. Gary knew he couldn't really force him and didn't want a wrestling match in the water out to sea, so Gary was winched back up into the helicopter. When back in the chopper the pilot said, "What's going on, where is he Gaz?"

Gary said, "He refuses to come with us. He's going to swim out himself down south somewhere." The pilot said (with a few swear words added), "You're joking aren't you? He's a fool."

Gary said, "How are we going for fuel?"

Pilot said, "Plenty of fuel. We'll go up, do circuits and watch him."

The crew carefully watched the man swimming. They were all really worried they would lose sight of him, which would be disastrous. A fatality was not an option for the crew. They came out in the chopper for a successful rescue, not a dead body recovery. They all felt the pressure and began snapping quietly at each other with questions,

"Have you still got visual?"

"What's his position now?"

"Where the hell is he?"

"Don't take your eye off him, will you?"

At one stage Gary saw a school of baitfish heading towards the shallow water. The lifesaver was near the school and Gary feared that a shark (or more) would be attracted to the fish and attack the lifesaver instead. Thankfully, no sharks were spotted. At one point Gary thought he might even make up a shark sighting to scare the lifesaver into coming in the chopper. He resisted that urge.

The lifesaver stopped swimming and began to tread water but then started swimming again in stops and starts for quite some time. The crew followed his every move using binoculars. The next thing Gary saw the man sink under the water and come up again. A frightening sequence began. Gary was saying to the pilot, "He's under. He's up. He's under. He's up. He's under."

Colour drained from Gary's face when he realised the lifesaver was in real trouble now as he hadn't surfaced. He urged the pilot to bring him closer to the water. The pilot told them to hang on and he tipped the helicopter onto its side, stalled the rotor disk and dropped out of the sky towards the ocean. He regained the hover just above the lifesaver and Gary used the momentum of the helicopter to jump from the skid into the water. Gary pulled the man to the surface by the hair. Exhausted, cold, coughing and vomiting sea water, the man was in a real hysterical panic, out of control. He was in survival mode and unaware of his surroundings and Gary's presence. Gary realised the man was now in a very poor condition. He needed not only rescue, but urgent medical intervention.

The lifesaver's arms were rotating vigorously in front of his chest. Gary looked under the water and saw the man's legs just hanging under him motionless. They'd given up with fatigue, his muscles full of acid. He was in his last throws of trying to stay afloat. Then Gary lost him in the swell. Gary's mind scrambled as he looked around above and below the water. Gary's heart raced as he realised he might lose him. He looked under water again and saw him. Gary took a huge deep breath, dived underneath the water and brought him to the surface. There was more coughing, gasping and vomiting. At this time, Gary was screaming at the man telling him to keep his arms still so that he could get a harness over him. He was locked out in a panic attack, not complying with Gary's orders. Mucus was coming out of his nose like a kid with the flu. He was staring at Gary with sheer panic in his eyes and attempting to grab him. Gary again screamed at him to keep his arms still, without success.

He began to sink again. In desperation, Gary dived under the water below him and finally got the harness up over his feet, drew it up his legs, around his body and finally under his armpits. He then brought them both to the surface. He clipped the lifesaver's harness onto his harness and inflated their lifejackets. That left Gary face to face with his 'foolish' lifesaver, but he was too exhausted himself to even have a go at the man for the trouble he'd caused.

Gary had to get his breath before the helicopter, which was overhead, lowered the winch wire down. Gary fastened on to the winch hook, he put both arms out and thumbs up to indicate he was ready and all was clear for the lift up into the aircraft. They were carefully hauled to safety onboard the helicopter. During the ascent into the chopper, the lifesaver rewarded Gary by vomiting lots of sea water all over him. Remember, they were face to face.

Gary laughed loudly and told me, "This is always a good incident to tell somewhere, especially just before a meal."

He continued to laugh before composing himself. This is Gary Raymond's personality. He always seems to get an appropriate laugh out of most things.

The lifesaver was flown back to a park near Bondi Beach where he was met by ambulance officers. They gave him oxygen therapy and wrapped him up in some space blankets (silver foil type blankets) as he was very much affected by the cold (hypothermia). His stomach still contained some salt water, so a trip to hospital was essential as salt water is not too good for your stomach, intestines or blood.

Gary and the crew were cleaning up the helicopter's equipment ready for the next mission when an Ambulance officer called across to him and said, "Hey Gaz, this bloke wants to see you before you lift off."

Gary went over to the man in the ambulance who said, through bloodshot eyes as he shivered, "I want to say I'm really sorry for the trouble I caused."

He grabbed Gary's hand with a tight squeeze, "Firstly, when you said I was in danger, I didn't believe you and take any notice. I was a proud fool. I thought I could do it. I was afraid my mates would ridicule me for having to get rescued by you blokes. I didn't want to be a laughing stock. What a fool I was."

He began to cry.

Gary reassuringly said, "That's alright mate, you're okay and that's the main thing. Just forgive yourself and move on."

He emotionally said, "Another thing: thank you for not leaving me out there. You could have left and gone back to base. I'm ever so grateful you didn't leave me there. You saved my life, I was drowning. I'll never forget you all."

Gary said decisively, "No way in the world we would have left you there, mate. We've never left anyone out there yet, and we're not starting now. You know, as a Christian cop this reminds me of something mate. Some people foolishly say, "I can make this life and eternity with my own beliefs, strength and skill without Jesus. Leave me alone God, I don't need you. God doesn't understand why we want to go it alone, when He's there to rescue us. Jesus said He is the only way to heaven, the only rescue method available to us (John 14:6). God says He loves us so much and doesn't want us to perish (2 Peter 3:9). God's going to stick around and when you put your hand up, like us in the chopper, He'll be right there waiting for you.

The lifesaver, who was still a bit teary said, "You're right. I need to get back to God and my church. This is a big wake-up call from God for me. Thanks for the reminder."

The ambulance took him to hospital. Gary found out he was in hospital for three days and recovered well. He is back with his church and growing to know Jesus better every day. He is still lifesaving and has joined the Australian Christian Surfer's Fellowship. It was a close call for him, however God was there providing a Police chopper and a dedicated crew to give him a second chance. Gary emotionally commented, "God is a specialist in giving people a second chance. After all, He gave me one."

The Gutter Drunk
About 9.00pm on a warm summer's night there was a serious collision on Parramatta Road, outside the Flemington Hotel. One

occupant was trapped inside the car and others were injured. Gary Raymond and his Police Rescue Squad arrived. After initial consultation with ambulance officers, it was noticed that the trapped driver had pressure on his chest by the caved in steering wheel causing breathing difficulties. This is a medical emergency so Gary got his rescue pocket-knife out and cut the rear part of the driver's seat open and removed the seat 'stuffing' which immediately allowed more space for the man to expand his chest and breathe. The driver was so grateful that he could now take deeper breaths although his chest was sore. What a relief!

At this point, a well intoxicated man in work clothes walked over from the nearby hotel to Gary. With slurred speech he asked, "I work for the railways and I've got my First Aid Certificate. Can I give you a hand, I know what I'm doing?"

Gary turned and said, "Thanks mate but it's alright. We have it under control. Move out of the way please, back over to the footpath." He returned a second time to Gary said, "I've got my Railway First Aid Certificate, you know. I can help."

Gary said sternly, "Look mate we are okay. Just go back out of the way now."

To say the least, this was most annoying for Gary as he was in the process of freeing the trapped man. The drunk came over a third time and as he did so, Gary noticed petrol flowing from the vehicle. The Fire Brigade was on the way.

Gary said to the drunk, "Yes, there is something you can do mate. Stop the petrol going down into the drain. The drunk walked over to the gutter, squatted down and put his hands together like a 'v' shaped dam to stop the petrol flowing down the drain. Gary panicked. He noticed the man had a cigarette in his mouth. Gary yelled out at the top of his voice, "Don't you light that cigarette; we'll all be blown up. The man calmly said, "No, I'm not going to light it. I never do. It just feels good in my mouth when I'm working and when I'm finished, I'll have it. I'm not that drunk that I'd blow myself up."

Gary finished the rescue and got the driver safely out of the car into an ambulance. The Fire Brigade had arrived, stopped the vehicle's petrol leak and assisted Gary and the ambulance officers. Gary had forgotten all about the drunk and the task he had delegated to the 'nuisance' of a man.

The Fire Brigade Station Officer said to Gary, "What's that bloke doing sitting in the gutter down the road?" Gary looked around only to see the drunk still sitting in the gutter; his hands remaining in the position to stop the petrol flow. Gary explained what he had told the man to do. Gary walked over to the man and said, "Thanks mate, you can go home now or back into the pub. The petrol flow has been stopped at the car." There was no response. Gary looked closer. To his utter amazement, the man was snoring. He was actually fast asleep sitting up in the gutter. When the Station Officer saw the cigarette still stuck to his lower lip, he was just about to yell out in horror when Gary quickly explained the man liked a smoke in his mouth and lit up when he finished a job. The officer shook his head in disbelief. Gary explained, "It's the only way I could get rid of him other than in the rear of a caged police truck."

The man was woken up and fire fighters decontaminated him of petrol. It was all over his trousers, especially in the crotch area. Gary arranged for a police car to take the man home. Gary laughed at the prospect of the drunk having to explain to his wife why he arrived home without trousers and underpants soaking wet with water. Gary doesn't know if, or when he finally got to have a cigarette after his kind deed for Gary at the collision.

Lightning Strikes the Force
There was a day during the Sydney 'storm season' when two Detective Sergeants walked into the Blacktown Police Station Detective's Office. They were Gary's mates. They entered via the back door. Nothing unusual about that except Gary noticed something was wrong. They glared at him with a half grin. One

detective pointed at Gary and said loudly, "It's your entire fault Gaza." The two men were pale and shaken. They were quiet and looked rather sheepish. One of them pointed upwards to the sky and proclaimed, "You've been talking to Him too much." Gary figured out they meant talking to God too much.

Gary said with jest, "So what's wrong with that?"

They then explained. "We were in the police car when suddenly the car got hit by a bolt of lightning. As we drove along the road there was a sudden flash and jolt on the car. We seemed to be enveloped for a second or two in a bubble of bright purple flame!"

Everyone in the office laughed.

Again, one of the Detective Sergeants looked at Gary, pointed upwards and said, "You've been talking to Him too much."

Gary said slowly, "Well gentlemen, it would be good if you gave your lives to Jesus today otherwise I might arrange another 'demonstration' from the sky!" All the cops in the office laughed, but the message was heard. The upside of the event was the fact the police car was not damaged and the two detectives not injured. After this event, the police were never quite sure of the connection Gary has with the Almighty and whether he was 'talking to Him too much'. Gary said confidently, "You can never talk to Him too much."

Taxi Driver in Attack Mode

A taxi driver, tired after his nightshift went home to Prospect, a Sydney suburb for a good 'day's' sleep. He woke with a startle to hear someone moving around in his house when nobody except him should be there. He quietly and slowly got out of bed and crept down the hallway to the lounge room. Much to his surprise, he saw a scruffy looking man, about 30 years old ratting through drawers in a cabinet. Enraged and scared, he charged the man and 'crash tackled' him. The two fought on the lounge, on the floor and against the walls. It was half a boxing match and half a wrestling match, which created a unique struggle. The fight moved quickly around the room as they embraced and locked onto each other.

Suddenly, they both fell through a plate glass sliding door onto the outside concrete verandah. The offender sustained some nasty cuts from the jagged glass, however miraculously, the taxi driver didn't even get a scratch. The wrestle vigorously continued on the verandah until finally the taxi driver restrained the offender and ended up sitting on top of him. He noticed a milk crate nearby containing some tools and an electric cord. He reached over and got the cord. He tied the offender's wrists together behind his back then gathered his ankles up to his wrists and tied them. Gary laughed and said, "It was the best 'hog-tying' job I've ever seen. Better than the Royal Easter Show rodeo cowboy display!"

By then the offender was well and truly tied up. The taxi driver decided that was not enough. How dare this man break into his house and try to steal his property.

He then got a piece of timber and began to beat the fellow along the whole length of his body, especially his backside. He also whipped him with the 'left over' end of the electric cord. When he'd finished doing him over, he phoned the police. When the patrolling police arrived, they took the timber off the taxi driver, untied the offender and called for an ambulance. They also called for detectives. Gary and his mate arrived. They saw the offender covered in cuts and bruises with marks up and down his body. Gary said, "He looked like he had just been in the middle of an explosion, as you see in cartoons like 'The Road Runner.'" The offender was transported to Blacktown Hospital and his wounds were stitched up. Gary has forgotten the number of stitches he received, but it took doctors hours to complete the job.

On the offender's discharge from the hospital, at the police station Gary faced a dilemma. The offender complained that the taxi driver had assaulted him. The question facing Gary and his mate was, did the taxi driver use excessive force in order to arrest and restrain the offender? Was it an unlawful assault? During the interview Gary asked the offender whether he wanted to take action against the taxi driver. He replied, "If I do, the Magistrate will have lots of sympathy towards the taxi driver as he was only protecting his possessions and I scared the life out of him. I suppose if someone had broken into my home, I would have done the same so I want to drop the complaint. Besides, Mr Raymond, if the boys in jail get to hear I was flogged by a mere taxi driver, they'll put dirt on me and will laugh their heads off and give me a hard time. Best if we forget it. Please don't tell anyone Mr Raymond."

Gary took a 'retraction statement' from the offender. He was charged with break, enter with intent to steal and a number of other related charges. He pleaded guilty and did three months jail for it. Gary grinned and jested, "I don't know what tall story he's going to sling the boys in jail to explain all his 'window glass' scars. I guess his story will be a very dramatic one that makes him out to be a hero."

Gary noted it's a highly emotional situation when you confront or attempt to disarm an offender in your own home or business. Day or night is just as risky. The encounter happens without much warning so you are caught by surprise, with the adrenalin pumping. You may fight, flight or freeze. It takes your brain a few seconds to calculate that you are under threat, especially at night, in the dark. You have to size up the situation quickly. It is a very dangerous time for the home or business occupier. Many questions have to be answered in a split second whilst you're under duress:
- Is the offender armed?
- Will the offender grab something of yours in the house to use as a weapon?
- Is the offender stronger than you?
- Will you sustain injury, or worse, in a physical encounter?

- Will more of your property be damaged in a physical encounter?
- Is the offender alone?
- Does the offender have a communicable disease?
- If you get defeated, will the offender harm other members of your family in the house?
- Will the offender tie you up and leave you unable to free yourself?
- Will the offender take a hostage in a bid to escape?
- Are you causing the offender to escalate their harm by blocking their escape route?
- How do you judge enough force to subdue such an offender in the heat of the moment?
- Do you have a 'force measuring instrument' that gives you a force reading?

The situation is unpredictable. Once you use force, then the offender uses more force to overcome what they perceive as a threat to their own wellbeing and so the situation can escalate. Gary further says, "The answer is to avoid physical confrontation with an offender unless forced to defend yourself and others. Remember, no property is worth dying or getting seriously injured for. The offender's escape must not be blocked. If possible, you retreat quickly away from the offender and escape yourself. Go outside and hide somewhere or go to a room, lock and barricade the door with furniture. Ring the Police on '000' (or the emergency number applicable to your country). Stay hidden until police presence is confirmed. Without jeopardising your safety, take note of the offender's description and don't touch anything enabling the scene to be preserved for fingerprint, shoe print, DNA, blood or other forensic evidence. After such an intrusive encounter, obtain professional support because spiritual, psychological and emotional disturbances may arise immediately, down the track or both."

The Under the Bed Dad
Gary knocked on the door of a house where a fellow lived who was wanted for questioning on a criminal offence. The man's wife came to the door. Gary showed his police identification and explained they were looking for her husband and said, "Can you tell us where he is?"

"No, I don't know," weas the response.

"Strange, for we had a report he lives here and is at home right now?"

"No, definitely not here, I'll go and get the address of where he might be."

Just when the woman left, a small child aged about three or four came to the door. Gary said, "Hello, what's your name?" then added, "Where's Daddy?"

There was an immediate response from the child, who said enthusiastically,

"He's under the bed."

"What bed?"

"His and mummy's bed."

The woman came back to the door and said,

"I couldn't find the address where he might be but if he comes here, I'll ring you straight away."

Gary replied sarcastically, "Oh, we found him."

"Oh, where?"

"He's under your bed."

She was startled and without thinking said, "How did you know he was under the bed?"

"We have our means to get information."

Gary and his mate then went to the main bedroom. Gary said loudly and sternly, "Come out mate or I'll come and get you. Or would you prefer I get a police dog to come and get you? Your choice." The suspect crawled out from under the bed. Gary handcuffed him and they transported him back to Blacktown Police Station.

Gary reflected on his little 'secret informant'. "Out of the mouth of babes and sucklings you get some great information." A lot of detectives ignore children at crime scenes but Gary says he takes a special note of what they say. He says, "It is often a snippet of a puzzle you need that an adult at the scene has forgotten or deliberately withholds from police. Children are more willing not to filter information like adults do. They don't measure the consequences of telling the facts as they saw them and become very excited when helping the police (unless their parents have taught them to hate the police). Children often stand back and see more than the adults intimately involved in the proximity of the incident. On school excursions, children are taught to take note of people and things. This skill flows over when they are reporting a crime."

Gary says, "Don't get me wrong; if they are the offender they can lie, exaggerate or trivialize their version. As an investigator, I always take time out to listen to the children. It's paid off many times and actually solved crimes. Children also need comforting, for they fall subject to the misdeeds of parents and others which hurt them physically, emotionally and spiritually as well. They suffer too with grief, critical incident stress and post traumatic stress as a result of an intrusive event in their lives or others around them. Jesus said to take notice of children and not harm them. He said not to look down on them as worthless (Matthew 18:10)."

The Persons of Interest Tree.
Gary received a call saying two young men had smashed the windows of a house while people were home in Kildare Road, Blacktown, then running off down the road. Quite a number of police went down and searched the area. A perimeter was formed. The police were confident the youths were still in the area, so they cordoned it off. The police searched high and low without success. They looked in storm water drains and every crook and cranny that was in the area. Gary called the police to his

location and enquired about their search. They assured him they had conducted a complete search. Gary made them search again, telling them the perimeter was secure and the POI (Persons of Interest) could not have got away. Gary saw the frustrated look in their eyes and on their faces but they were not game enough to backchat their Duty Officer. They searched again with no result. A police dog and handler arrived and began tracking the offenders. The dog went around the area. Finally, the dog handler said, "We lost the track here somewhere. I think they have either got away on a bicycle or in a car." The police again reported to Gary the search had been unsuccessful. Gary gathered all the police around him.

Gary in a calm manner announced, "Ladies and gentlemen, please look up into the tree that we are standing under."

They all looked up in unison. To their surprise, there they were. The two offenders perched up in the old gum tree like startled koalas being illuminated by about 10 police torches. They were ordered to come down. There was a noise in the tree leaves. Two youths scurried down out of the branches down the trunk and into the arms of the waiting police. Gary at this point was rather annoyed that not one of the police officers present for the search had tracked down the youths up in the tree. Gary did. He had spotted the two in the tree when he first arrived and remained under the tree all the time the search was underway. Gary was 'testing' his staff to see whether they would eventually find them. Gary recalled his early Police Rescue Squad training the Sergeants instilled in them all that when conducting search and rescue to always look around all dimensions. Up, down and around. Gary then told those gathered, "Whenever you search for offenders or lost people, look around, up and beneath you." He told them there always needs to be a three dimensional search because the world is not flat, like some in our past history thought.

So ends the story of the POI tree. Gary says, "That's the way the valuable lessons of policing are passed down the line, over the years, to the less experienced officers who then pass them on to their subordinates. Gary chuckling said, "Even now when I see some of those who were there that night. They walk up to me, look upwards and remind me they haven't forgotten the lesson. I'm proud of them and my lesson was not in vain."

King Hit

These days it seems we constantly hear about 'king hits' or 'coward punches' and we are subject to story after story of the sad result of such common attacks. Back at the time when Gary was a Probationary Constable at Redfern, he learned a tough lesson about king hits.

It was a quiet night when Gary was on a routine patrol in a paddy wagon (caged police truck) with a Sergeant around the suburb of Redfern (just south of the City of Sydney). It was closing time for the hotels. All of the pubs in Redfern had a bad reputation for drunkenness, brawling and damage to property, which is unlike these days with all the new strategies to minimise these behaviours. Often drunks left cranky because they were told to leave at closing time. Referring to their last drinks, the licensee of the pub would yell out, "If you can't finish them leave them, and if you can't leave them finish them!"

At the time, Gary and his Sergeant kept their eyes on the Empress Hotel. Publicans appreciated a police presence. As the two police watched, the publican at the Empress came out of his pub, saw the police and told them he had trouble clearing patrons from his pub.

His plea: "Some of the drinkers are refusing to leave. Can you help?"

The two police entered the pub and the people started to leave. However, one fellow was sitting in a chair, bent forward with his forehead resting on his folded hands as he slept at a table. The Sergeant ordered, "Wake him up and throw him out, Gary."

"Yes Serg," Gary replied obediently.

Gary walked over to the man and vigorously shook his left shoulder and said loudly,

"Come on mate time to go home. Wake up. Come on, get up and get out of here."

The next thing Gary remembers, he felt pain in the jaw and became a little bit dizzy, immediately seeing stars. He shook his head, stayed on his feet and realised he had been 'king hit' by this man from the sitting position. The fellow, now wide-awake, stood up in front of him. Gary had been punched directly in the jaw.

The man took another swing at Gary, which Gary blocked. Gary grabbed the man's wrist, swept his legs out from under him with his foot and threw him to the ground, twisting his arm up his back as he went. Gary then wrist locked the man, turned him over flat on his stomach and handcuffed him. At this stage Gary was still a little dizzy from the punch and as he says still 'seeing a few stars'. His head was ringing and his jaw was sore.

After gaining his composure, Gary made the man stand on his feet, marched him out of the pub (his feet hardly touching the ground) and into the rear of the paddy wagon. This particular 'king hit' man was charged with assaulting a police officer. Later in court, he was found not guilty of the charge because the Magistrate said that the man didn't know Gary was a police officer and thought it was someone trying to hit him or steal from him. Self defence, they reckoned. The Magistrate said, "Constable Raymond should have announced his office so the defendant realised it was a police intervention."

Gary disagreed, but that's the law. However, because there were outstanding warrants for the man's arrest, he was brought back into custody and went to jail for a lengthy sentence. There is justice after all it's added up. A good arrest for Gary, even though it was achieved the hard way.

One thing the incident did was to heighten Gary's reflexes. His past meddling in boxing and karate sure helped him to sustain the blow. What a lesson Gary Raymond learned that night. Some drunks are like mousetraps: they go 'snap' with the slightest touch, and go off wildly swinging at whoever and whatever might be near. Gary learned that in the future it was best to give a drunk a gentle poke with a baton from a distance than standing too close. He was never caught napping again, for that was the first and last time he received a "king hit' while serving in the force. Once bitten, twice shy would sum it up!

Trapped by a Crusher
When Gary was working at Cabramatta Police Station, the Vietnamese immigrants had transformed many of the shops serving food and drink with a real Asian authentic cuisine. Noodle soups with flavours so succulent you can't stop eating them. A number of shops had a machine with a drum and roller for crushing the juice out of fresh sugar cane. The Vietnamese made sweet drinks from the cane juice by this process. You may add orange juice and ice to make a great drink. On patrol, Gary and his mates would stop and buy a drink, especially in the middle of a hot summer's day.

One day a triple '0' call came in. Someone was trapped in a machine in a food shop. It was soon revealed that a Vietnamese child had been feeding sugar cane into one of the machines when his fingers were pulled in between the rollers. He was well and truly trapped. The grandfather immediately stopped the machine, hearing shrieks from the child. When Gary arrived, the grandfather suggested he reverse the machine's rollers to bring the boy's fingers out backwards. Gary strongly disagreed to this suggestion, as his Police Rescue Squad days told him you could double the damage and disturb blood clotting by reversing machinery back over trapped body parts. The machine had to be dismantled. Ambulance and Police Rescue were on the way. Gary began to dismantle the machine using tools from a nearby tradesman's kit pending arrival of help. An ambulance arrived and the child was given pain relief and oxygen therapy. The machine was dismantled by Police Rescue and the rollers carefully separated. The child's fingers and hand were carefully lifted off the lower roller, bandaged and splinted. He was taken to hospital. Because of this type of incident, the Workcover Authority inspectors went to the shop to check the machine and find the cause of the injuries. The owner was in strife because of the child's age working in the shop. Doctors performed microsurgery on the child and he was in hospital for six days followed by a long rehabilitation and physiotherapy program.

Some 12 months after the incident, Gary was walking past the shop where the boy was injured. He went into the shop and saw the grandfather. Gary said, "How's your grandson after the accident with the sugar cane crusher?"

"He alright, he's much better, no trouble for him."

He took Gary to the back of the shop and he saw his grandson. Gary was shocked. The boy was working on the same crusher. He was feeding sugar cane into the machine with his good hand. His injured hand had healed well but displayed scarring from the injury and subsequent surgery.

Gary surprised said, "He might get caught again, mightn't he?"

"Oh no Mr Gary," came the reply. "He will never get caught like that again."

"This is not good Sir. If you continue to use him, I will have to report you to Workcover. Do you understand that?" The grandfather immediately took the boy away from the machine and told him not to work on it again. Gary left the shop shaking his head in disbelief.

It occurred to Gary that government agencies need to educate immigrants prior to their arrival, or shortly thereafter, on the Workplace Health & Safety laws in Australia. There's a huge difference between the laws here and overseas, especially in third world or underdeveloped countries. Ignorance of safe work practices costs lives, causes injuries and is accompanied by high economic costs as well.

"They shouldn't learn by mistakes, they should have learnt how to prevent such mistakes," Gary told me.

Walking On Broken Glass

When Gary and Michelle Raymond were living at Prospect, they were disturbed in the early hours of the morning. Noises were coming from their backyard shed. Gary got out of bed and crept to the back window. He left the lights off. He saw what appeared to be a man helping himself to tools in his shed.

Prior to this, Gary had noted that there was a car out the front of his house with its engine idling. Gary worked out it was the offender's get-away vehicle (probably stolen) ready for a quick escape. Gary thought if he went to the back door the offender would escape over the back fence and get away. Gary decided to go out quietly in the dark via the front door and hide behind some shrubs. He was getting himself ready to jump on the offender as he came down the side of the house to get to the car. Since time was of the essence, Gary was still in his underpants (or what he calls 'summer pyjamas') having had no time to dress.

A short time later the man came down the side of Gary's house and at the right moment and distance, Gary took a massive leap towards the offender. Unfortunately, Gary's right shoulder and arm hit a shrub branch making a noise. This startled the thief who dropped his stolen property and ran towards his car with Gary in close foot pursuit.

The thief then realised he wouldn't make it to his car, so he went around the back of it, crossed the road and attempted to jump the back fence of a neighbour's house opposite. Gary tried to grab the thief by the back of his clothes, but to no avail. He kicked and Gary lost his grip. As the man landed on the other side of the fence, Gary heard a dull grinding, crunching, crumbling sound. It was an unusual eerie sound, hard for Gary to describe.

It was followed by, "Oh, oh, oh, oh, please help me."

Gary went to the end of the fence and as he looked across to where the man was Gary was slightly amused (but kept a straight face) to discover the barefoot man had jumped onto a big pile of empty 'long neck' beer bottles that had been placed in cardboard

cartons. The cartons were all soggy and wet due to rain. The man's weight had caused his feet to break through the cartons, which had been stacked three boxes high. His feet went from top to bottom of the stack of cartons. The man was yelling in discomfort caused by his entrapment,
"Please help me, please help me."
Gary quickly frisked the man for weapons as he was begging to be pulled out from the glassy mess. Every time the man moved, broken glass stuck into his skin and gave him an extra cut. Each wriggle made him sink lower into the glass. something like glass 'quick sand.'
Gary yelled, "Stay still mate. I'll work out how to get you out without further damage." The man was by this time screaming in excruciating pain, begging Gary to hurry.
At this point, other neighbours woken by all the noise came to Gary's assistance. Gary and two other men lifted the man upwards out of the pile of broken glass by grabbing him under the armpits and around his thighs, then laying him on the grass. Since the man was bleeding quite badly and still whimpering in pain, a neighbour got some towels. Gary was not able to wrap the towels around the man too tightly because of the shards of glass in the soles of his feet and all the way up his legs to his thighs, sticking into him. Some shards Gary was able to safely remove but he wasn't game to tackle the larger shards in case he caused further injury and bleeding. He put direct pressure on the bleeding that did not have any impacted glass in it. He elevated his limbs, again to minimise blood loss. Certainly, Gary's training as an ambulance officer came to the fore.
Even though Gary was amused, he still maintained a straight face. He thought of the messy situation and how justice comes in many guises. A short time later, the police and ambulance arrived and the offender was taken to Blacktown Hospital under police guard. Gary got dressed and went to the hospital with the police. The offender received 54 stiches in his wounds during time in the operating theatre. His wounds were washed out before the

sutures were put in. Later, Gary laughed when the doctor told him exactly how many stiches were placed in the man. The doctor also laughed when Gary explained how the whole incident came about. Gary says he will never forget the number of stitches. It would have been better if the offender gave in to Gary's arrest. The police told Gary that the car left running out the front of his house had been reported stolen. The man was charged with breaking, entering, theft and car theft. After the man came out of hospital, he was taken to the police station and charged.

Gary said, "Unfortunately, there is no charge on the statute books for committing a foolish getaway."

The offender was not charged with malicious damage for breaking the bottles. The neighbour said jesting, "I'll put the bottles in for recycling, in many pieces instead of whole bottles."

There was a joke at the police station when the offender was charged. When people are arrested and charged, their scars and tattoos are updated on their criminal record for identification purposes. Gary told the Station Sergeant, "Don't forget to record his scars and tattoos.

The Sergeant belligerently said to Gary, "I'll be all blinking day recording his new scars."

Gary doesn't know what became of the man, but guarantees in the future he'll sure look before he leaps!

Body in Drain

The scene was the Cooks River Canal. A call had gone out to general duty police and ambulance crews that a man's body had been seen floating in the canal. The body needed recovering. Who better than the elite Police Rescue Squad? In those days industry along the canal was less conscientious regarding the release of chemicals and oil into waterways. Pollution was common and was not inspected like it is today. When Gary arrived with the rescue team, he was faced with a dirty polluted canal from which his task was to retrieve a floating body. The body was floating face down. Gary always wore swimming trunks under his rescue overalls, as going into water or getting wet on rescues was common. Gary took off his overalls and was lowered into the canal where the water height was up to shoulder level. Still wearing his rescue boots as the bottom of the canal was covered in sharp rubbish, he walked out from the edge of the canal to the floating body.

On reaching the body, he tied a rope around it and kept it afloat while his team pulled it to the wall of the canal. A stokes litter (which was like a basket stretcher made of a steel frame with wire sides) was placed in the water and Gary placed it under the body. While Gary supported the litter, it was pulled to the edge of the canal and lifted up onto the grass verge. Gary was then assisted up the side of the canal out of the water by his mates. After Forensic examination, Gary and his mates placed the body into a zipped up body bag.

Gary told me, "Body recovery was one of the tasks of Police Rescue. Many were in a state of decomposition or burnt. We recovered them from all sorts of places. Rooftops, ceilings, basements, under buildings, waterways, bush areas, base of cliffs, under trains or even exhuming buried bodies from murder scenes. Talk about 'dust to dust and ashes to ashes'; we saw it all. It showed us how vulnerable the human body is when left to the elements. It was a tough job but we switched off and detached from the sights, smells and touches of death, looking at it from a police investigative point of view. Besides all that, this body was once a person that had family and friends. In Police Rescue, we were taught to handle dead bodies with respect, which we did. As a Christian, I understand what the Bible says about death. Trusting in Christ, when we die, we will later get a new body suited to living in eternity with God on the new 'renovated' earth." (Revelation 21:1)

The body from the canal was then examined and photographed by forensic officers, placed in a body bag, and transported to the city morgue. It was discovered on autopsy that the man had suffered a heart attack when walking alongside the canal and fallen into the water where he drowned. There were no suspicious circumstances.

Meanwhile, Gary found he was covered from the shoulders down by a blackish, brownish sludge. They had water aboard the rescue truck and Gary's team tried, without success, to wash him down. In spite of the best efforts by Gary and his mates, only the 'gooey' stuff on the skin surface came away from his body. Gary told his mates he'd go back to the rescue station and get the rest off in the shower. Shower he did, but to his horror, the pollutant had impregnated the pores of his skin like a tattoo. He used soap and detergent to try and remove the pigment without success.

A couple of the rescue blokes tried detergent and scrubbing brushes to rub Gary down, again without success. One of the Sergeants suggested they should try turpentine or kerosene, but they didn't work either. It only made Gary's skin red and irritated without removing the pigmentation. It was then decided to take Gary down to the South Sydney Hospital to seek the advice of a Dermatologist. After several attempts by doctors and nurses to remove the pigment, it was decided to put hot packs on Gary's skin and then place him in a hot bath to open the pores of his skin.

Again the stains remained. Nurses used skin lotions with very hard towels in further attempts to get rid of the pollution stains. Again, they failed. The doctors then phoned a number of petroleum and engineering companies seeking to find out what they use for such a case. A chemical engineer from the University of New South Wales was summoned to the hospital. He suggested an acetone liquid be used. However, that was ruled out by another doctor who said the chemical might burn or further irritate Gary's skin. All this time Gary's skin was already red and swollen from all the cleaning activity.

The doctor directed that Gary go home and come back in a couple of days when the skin inflammation had settled down. Gary didn't go home but stayed on duty at the rescue station. No way was he going off on 'sick report' with this. There were rescues to be done and his mates to be backed up. He was sore and uncomfortable but that didn't stop him fronting up.

Gary became most concerned that the tattooing effect might last a lifetime. He returned to the hospital and the doctor said he'd consulted with Dermatologists in America and Britain, who said there was nothing that could get rid of the pigmentation. Only the new skin cells would grow upwards and replace the pigmented ones which would drop off. Over the ensuing weeks, Gary's skin gradually rid itself of the offending pollutant particles. He ceased being known as the 'tattooed policeman'. Thankfully, these days the Cooks River Canal and many more waterways are no longer polluted since the EPA (Environmental Protection Authority) has come down heavily on polluters and thankfully, good waterway management prevails.

Gary said, "The whole episode reminded me that the 'stain' of our sin cannot be removed by anything except the precious cleansing blood of Jesus which was spilt for us when He died on the cross at Calvary (Isaiah 1:18). I'm so glad that even though I fail God every day, my sin and its stains are washed away completely so that in God's sight, I'm spotless."

A Detective Discovers Truth Pays

A detective planned to lie in court. Gary had been on night shift, however he had to stay at work to go to court in the morning. He went down to the custody cell area to speak to an offender.

Whilst he was there, another offender from an adjoining cell said to Gary, "One of your detectives is going to lie in court. He's going to say that I did a job on a house breaking when he knows I didn't do that one. He said he wanted to clear it up and I had to wear it anyway. I did a heap of others Mr Raymond which I told him about, but not that one."

Gary found the detective and confronted him. He told Gary, "Well he's done one, he's done the lot. He can wear it."

It appeared the detective in question was going to stick him for a crime he didn't commit. Gary said, "That's not right mate. If you do that, you'll cause me to inform the Prosecutor."

"Yes mate, thanks for that," the officer replied. "If you do that I'll lose my job and I'll be on the street. My wife and kids will suffer."

"Don't blame me mate, you're the one doing the wrong thing, not me. You wouldn't expect your kids to lie to you so don't you lie in court. You're on oath mate, or doesn't that mean much to you?"

The case concerning this was third up. Gary went into court and sat waiting for his case to come up. Two cases came up. Gary was so tired after night shift he didn't take much notice of the evidence being given. Then the Prosecutor offered no evidence on the third matter. Gary realised the detective must have told the Prosecutor to withdraw it. Gary's case was short, so he then went to the back of the court and asked where the detective was. "Oh, he's gone home on sick report."

Gary called in to see the detective on his way home. He said, "Just wanted to see how you were."

"I dropped the matter."

"How come?"

"Well you were sitting on a seat in the court, arms outstretched ,head down. (Gary had a beard and was in plain clothes). When I looked at you the sun shone through the window on you. It reminded me of Jesus Christ on the cross. This then reminded me that if I said anything untrue I'd be lying in the sight of God. As a result I spoke to the Prosecutor during the adjournment of the case."

The detective looked at Gary and said, "I promise you I'll never go through that again. Will you tell Jesus I'm sorry?"

Gary told him, "You can tell Jesus personally for when He died the veil of the temple was torn in two and He made forgiveness possible. It's not what we've done to Him, it's what He's done for us."

The detective said, "I've not only jeopardised my job but my family and future. I'll never do it again. I was so angry. I'm sorry Gaz for putting you in that situation. Thank you for being so strong and having the guts to confront me over it. It wasn't comfortable but I needed it. That's what mates are for."

CHAPTER THREE

TANGLED WAYS

"Oh what a tangled web we weave, when first we practice to deceive." Sir Walter Scott (Novelist)

Part One: Shockwaves

Are you ready for a shock? Can you imagine for one minute, serving police officers committing the following crimes?

- Takes cash bribes from drug dealers
- Steal money and drugs whilst executing search warrants
- Sharing stolen money with other corrupt police
- Allowing drug dealers to keep drugs and money during search warrants
- Arrange drug rip-offs
- Hide stolen money in jars under your parent's house without their knowledge
- Sell your police identification badge to a drug dealer to pretend they're a police officer and conduct rip-offs of competing dealers
- Falsifying (verballing) records of interview with suspects.
- Assaulting suspects in interview rooms
- Conducting and arranging 'home invasions'
- Selling illegal drugs
- Loading up suspects with drugs to charge them with possession
- Falsifying information to obtain search warrants

- Steal money before exhibit photographs
- Fake 'hurt on duty' and falsify claims
- Steal property exhibits
- Falsify evidence to obtain illegal money back from police custody
- Purchase expensive items with 'bribe money'
- Build home extensions with 'bribe money'
- Use police credit cards to fill your own car with fuel
- Obtain private & confidential information from the police computer system to give to criminals
- Send corrupt police into the police assessment centres to obtain privileged information on the police promotion system for unfair promotion advantage

(*Sydney Morning Herald*, **4 May 2002**)
"Corrupt Manly detective Sergeant Raymond John Peattie was jailed for three years two months last night for accepting bribes from other corrupt police on the Northern Beaches who allegedly robbed or exhorted money from criminals. The former Crime Manager at Manly Police Station was sentenced to a total of eight years' imprisonment, but District Court Judge Michael Finnane found Peattie warranted a substantial discount in his sentence because he had not only admitted his guilt but been honest and provided fresh evidence on other corrupt police."

The time came when it was revealed to the New South Wales Police Commissioner that part of his police force was rotten to the core. The fact was deep corruption. The truth was many police were involved. The truth had to be revealed for as Frank Wright (1860-1959) said, "The Truth is more important than the facts".

Imagine the Commissioner of Police in New South Wales at that time, Peter Ryan, sitting in his plush office and receiving a report of corruption at one of his main two police stations, Manly and Dee Why on the shores of Sydney's Northern Peninsula. See him as he ponders a replacement. The Manly post has become empty due to the incumbent Commander's emotional ill health.

Ryan scans the list of possible replacements, sees the name of Acting Inspector Gary Raymond, and mutters to himself, "Hmmm, a Christian cop. Why not drop him into the post. But I'll say nothing of the corruption. Let's see how he works things out. We'll keep it secret and use him as an experiment, a 'laboratory rat' as it were."

Gary still can't believe that a Commissioner of Police would send a new Commander to a station knowing that it was riddled with corruption and not tell him. It's like sending a Captain to a ship knowing it had a major leak and not telling him. It was as bad as sending police into an ambush that you knew about and didn't warn them. Gary wonders if it wasn't some sort of game Ryan was playing with his people.

Was this the scenario into which Gary Raymond was dropped? Maybe this is not too far from the truth. We will never know Ryan's motives for not telling Gary. Even after the corruption was exposed, Ryan never explained his motives to Gary. Knowing Manly Police Station was going under, did Ryan decide Gary Raymond had the ability to successfully take control? Did Ryan believe Gary Raymond would stop the corrupt dealings at Manly? Maybe we'll never know what was in Ryan's mind.

Gary took up as Officer in Charge of the Manly Local Area Command in November 1998. Unbeknown to Gary, a number of his Detectives were running with local drug dealers, making lots of money in the process. One of the corrupt detectives (whose name has been suppressed by the courts) full of fear and self preservation turned informant for the Police Integrity Commission (PIC). He made a deal to escape the consequences of his own corruption and agreed to gather voice recordings of corrupt cops on a hidden sound recorder strapped to his body under his clothing. Warrants were also obtained to record phone conversations at the Manly Police Station.

The corruption investigation caused the creation of 'Mascot' which had an off-shoot named 'Operation Florida'. To quote the official report to the New South Wales Parliament,

"The Commission's Operation Florida investigation arose from a joint NSW Crimes Commission, NSW Police investigation codenamed 'Mascot' which commenced early in 1999. The Commission joined the investigation in July 2000, by which time a substantial body of evidence of serious police corruption had been gathered by the officers from the NSW Crime Commission and the NSW Police Special Crime Unit."

Little did Gary know that when he was appointed to Manly his second in command, Ray Peattie, was to one day confess he was seriously corrupt. The date when the Sydney *Daily Telegraph* would print the following statement was still down the track and yet to be revealed.

"Police Commissioner Peter Ryan has unveiled his latest weapon in the fight against police corruption in NSW— corrupt Manly detective Ray Peattie." (5/12/2001)

Back on 26th August 2001, *Channel Nine News* Sydney had reported:

"The NSW Police and their Commissioner Peter Ryan have had a turbulent time over the past 12 months. They ended the Olympics last September with nothing but praise, but it's been a sharp downhill ride ever since crime figures suddenly shot up, a damning report from independent auditors highlighted the snail's pace of reform and the force was slammed by a parliamentary inquiry for its failure to effectively police crime-ridden Cabramatta."

Any wonder Peter Ryan left the job two years early!

Peattie who joined the force in 1977 admitted:

"Through my corrupt and thoughtless behaviour I have tarnished the reputation of the many fine and honest police and public servants." Peattie had held the rank of Detective Sergeant. He cooperated with investigators and made admissions about various corrupt activities in which he had been involved. At one stage he was asked what he thought a Crime Manager in the position he occupied should do to prevent corrupt conduct. He said, "Do the opposite of what I did."

TANGLED WAYS

It turned out Peattie was one of Peter Ryan's weapons to deal with corruption at Manly Police Station. It worked for Ryan as he used Peattie to 'dob' in other police who were corrupt. Peattie turned turtle and revealed much of what had been happening in the cesspit of police corruption known as the Manly Police Station. As is always the case, there were those who desired to make someone a scapegoat and pile all their vengeance on that one person, as if corruption as wide spread as the Manly affair could have been laid at the feet of one person.

To this day, there are those who argue there was undue delay in bringing the crook cops to justice. Some say they were allowed to operate way beyond any logical or safe time frame. Just imagine for years crooked cops armed with guns were allowed under the watchful eye of Ryan and surveillance police to operate with armed drug dealers. A deadly war could have erupted at any time between the corrupt police and the drug dealers. Thankfully for the community on this occasion, the relationship between the corrupt cops and the dealers was friendly. They were 'mates'. They cooperated with each other to make loads of money from human addiction and misery.

Gary said, "How a gun fight or physical fights didn't arise between the two groups is a miracle. They were allowed to operate for far too long by Ryan. Turf warfare was a possibility, conflict over money and drugs that could have caused murder or serious injury. A bit like we see today with the shootings between the rival gangs around Sydney. The corrupt cops and drug dealers had almost become one family at Manly mutually benefiting each other with money.

"In the past, during Roger Rogerson's era, corrupt cops had become enemies with those giving them bribe money. Constant tension and conflict was seen between the corrupt cops and the Kings Cross criminals. Stand over tactics from both sides. Guns were often produced as intimidation. Threats of death or serious injury were common. People were murdered and property damaged. The famous paper bag full of money was the prize.

Free meals, free grog, free drugs, free sex shows, free prostitutes, gambling premises and free holidays for the corrupt cops was another benefit in addition to large amounts of cash in those days. If criminals and drug dealers didn't give money to the corrupt cops, they risked getting 'loaded up' with trumped up criminal charges or valuable property taken from them like wrist watches and gold jewellery. It wasn't unusual to see bashings and threats of murder occur for bribe or protection money, especially if the payments were late. People gossiped about what they saw making rumours common and open."

Not the case at Manly. Totally opposite. The Manly corruption arrangements were friendly and sometimes even apologetic between the corrupt cops and drug dealers. No room for greed in this incestuous relationship as everyone was getting a fair share of the dirty money. Be kind and patient if the money was late or drugs had to be sold to get that money. Relax, the money will come. Don't create waves; the flow of tainted money was smooth and regular. It is what Gary called a 'mutual benefit society'. You give me money and you won't get arrested very often.

Let's look back to the time when Raymond was appointed to Manly. Gary reveals, "My first reaction when told I was commanding Manly was 'you beauty.' Commanding a police station in the sand, sea and sun. Reward for all the hard work I'd done over the years. I was thrilled to bits. After all I'd always been stationed at front line places like Redfern, Rescue Squad, Blacktown and Cabramatta, but now Manly, surely a crown in the jewel of police appointments."

Gary thought, "Somewhere a bit easier. What a change. After all, I've always been in the 'firing line' of policing. I didn't for one minute think it was going to turn into a nightmare. I realised it would mean extra travel between home and Manly, but I didn't mind as they provided an unmarked police car for Commander's who were on call to attend major crimes or other emergency management situations. Manly had its policing issues with licensed premises, drunken backpackers and beach crime, but nothing like the previous stations I'd been working. Michelle and I could have the occasional fish and chips on the Corso near the beach after work. This is a bonus after serving in some of the toughest police stations. It was as if Santa Claus had called at my door with a wonderful, specially packaged Christmas gift from Mr Ryan."

On the other, hand what a challenge! Gary knew the Manly area had issues, but he understood they were surface issues. He never dreamt of underhanded issues. He knew there were plenty of tourists visiting the area, especially by ferry and many rich people lived in the area. He felt very confident he was up to the challenge. He'd grown up with challenges since he entered the force, especially in the Rescue Squad. As the new Commander, Gary felt he could make a positive contribution in his new appointment.

Little did Gary realise that Peter Ryan, the Police Commissioner, was placing him in a hot spot. Sun, surf, sea, and sand yes, but what about the worms in the police system? Ryan knew of the corruption but said absolutely nothing to Gary. Not even a hint. As a lamb before wolves, Gary walked into the most corrupt police station in the history of the New South Wales Police Force. Those who were devious in his new charge must have smirked at his appointment. After all, they knew all the tricks of the trade. They knew Gary would be totally unsuspecting unless he saw evidence of something 'fishy' happening. Why even his second in command was on the fiddle. How could Gary have possibly guessed Ray Peattie was corrupt? You can't judge a book by its cover.

Once in position, the car drive to and from work didn't daunt Gary. Afterall, the 2000 Olympics were coming up with the promise of plenty of tourists visiting the 'sands of Manly'. Gary only had to ensure his troops were doing their job. He felt like a Roman Centurion with a trusty band of soldiers in his charge. On the first morning of his new charge, Gary flipped his cap on the hook in his new office, sat behind the desk, sipped his first cup of Manly coffee, looked out the window and muttered to himself that life is good. After all, he'd arrived at last. He quickly stopped dreaming and knuckled down to work meeting with staff, checking the Command's crime reduction status, finances, human resources and the rest of the vast areas of is responsibility on his plate. Unknown to him, there swirled all around him crooked people carrying a police badge. A core of cops as rotten as could be found across Australia.

The corridors of power contained the seeds of destruction and were indeed a trap for the unwary. Gary saw no outwards sign of this. Even his vast experience as a Senior Internal Affairs qualified Investigator, his Detective's designation and general knowledge of people didn't pick up signs of corruption. As with most jobs, the first glance can make any new appointment seem for a moment, like the first day of a delightful new experience. This is the time when most of us put on rose coloured spectacles.

Meanwhile in regard to another matter, namely beach theft, Gary introduced high profile policing. He introduced ATV (All Terrain Vehicles) to patrol public places. They were four wheelers that could take police anywhere. On the beach, in car parks, up and down stairs, in public parks, in bush and cross the area of Manly reservoir.

This new ATV idea was the first of its kind for policing in Sydney. Gary had them registered to drive on public streets, again a first in NSW. It gave police an advantage when finding and chasing crooks. The ATV went where other modes of police transport couldn't go. It also helped lifesavers and ambulance officers to carry injured people across the sand. The vehicles gave a much smoother ride and were a blessing for people with spinal injuries. Such vehicles also helped tourists.

Of tourists Gary says, "I came to realise young tourists visiting Manly broke every rule in the book. They'd come to Australia, grab a surfboard, jump into the water, attempt to hang ten and do all kinds of tricks along the green tunnel of waves at

Manly Beach. Sadly, many ended up flat on their backs gasping for breath. Lifesavers had to pick up the pieces. The tourists also caused 'surf rage' when their newly hired surfboards, with first time riders, would collide with local surfers on boards or swimming.

"They would stray into the 'flagged area' causing havoc amongst swimmers. Tourists would also cause 'skate board rage' by losing control of their skateboards and colliding with pedestrians along the promenade. Some ball games were prohibited on the beach. There were designated areas for beach volley ball only. Again tourists would play soccer or cricket, kicking up sand and hitting people with stray balls ('ball rage'). Fights sometimes broke out requiring police attendance for all of the 'types of rages'. Yet another headache for police and ambulance officers in Manly."

It didn't take Gary long to discover beach theft was particularly high. Gangs communicating with mobile phones prowled around looking for victims. When someone entered the water, one thief from an 'observation spot' on the Manly promenade would ring an accomplice on the beach. The thief on the beach then dug a hole in the sand and hid the swimmer's bag in the hole under their towel. When the swimmer came out of the water, they'd discover their bag was missing. They'd go to the police station or the lifeguard tower to report it. While they were away reporting the theft, the thieves would dig up the bag, take the money out of it and rebury it making off with their new found cash and jewellery. Very clever until Gary's beach patrol team got onto it and put a stop to them and their devious methods.

Another method used by thieves was to create a diversion. They'd say to their victim, "I think your name was just called over the public address system."

"How do you know my name?"

"What's your name?"

When they gave their name the response was, "Yes, that's the name they called out."

Either that or they'd listen for their name being used in general talk on the beach. The person would walk up to the life guard tower to see what was wanted and the thieves would make off with their money. Drunk or drugged people's property on the beach was also very easy pickings for thieves as the victim slept off their intoxicants, unaware of the theft.

One gang offered 'free surfboard riding lessons' to unsuspecting tourists. Whilst in the water 'under instruction', an accomplice would steal their money and on occasions, their passports too. Another theft scam was the offender would target tourists and take them up the beach away from their belongings on the pretence that he would show them a place to see and swim with beautiful tropical fish. Whilst away, another offender would steal belongings, especially cash.

All of these scams caused lots of anguish for our visitors, putting a nasty taste in their mouth about their long-anticipated holiday to Australia. The anguish was doubled when a camera was stolen containing images of their entire holiday up to that point in time. Just like photo albums being lost or destroyed in fire, floods, tornados or computer crashes, an irreplaceable and permanent loss. Such clever ploys were thwarted when Gary introduced a security trailer with locked pigeonholes onto the beach, run by a local businessperson. This meant swimmers had a safe place to leave their valuables, for a small cost.

Gary also introduced uniformed and plainclothes police to conduct foot patrols along the beach being both proactive and reactive. These police on patrol warned bathers of the dangers of theft and told them to be careful of their belongings. They also prevented anti-social behaviour, drinking or drug use on the beach. He also placed police on top of nearby high-rise buildings with binoculars. They conducted surveillance on thieves on the beach.

These crime reduction tactics by Gary caused a huge reduction in beach theft. He was applauded by the Regional Commander for his strategies in lowering the theft rate throughout the whole Command.

Police were both visible and mobile. Gary Raymond was indeed a knight in shining armour. For Gary 'all was right with the world and Manly'. Nothing could have been further from the truth. Underneath, it was more like paradise lost. He was totally unaware his second in command (crime manager) Ray Peattie and a number of his detectives were rotten to the core. Their methods were corrupt and very sneaky. They were comrades in underhanded crime and worse still, the whole bunch had tricks galore up their sleeves.

Of considerable interest is the way Peattie later responded to questions about Raymond's leadership as Commander of the Manly Police Station. He was complimentary. Later, he was to emotionally apologise to Gary and his wife for the harm he'd caused. With tears in his eyes Peattie told Gary, "I'm so sorry mate for the stuff I am putting you and Michelle through. I've wrecked your life and career. You are such a good bloke and great boss, but I've done the dirty on you."

Gary told me that Ray Peattie was genuine in his apology and conveyed real regret for his corruption. Gary forgave him and prayed for him. Gary even offered to help his family whilst he was in jail.

Gary told me, "It wasn't hard for me to forgive him as he was the one going to jail, not me. Jesus has forgiven all of my sins, so I forgave Peattie his sins against me. If we don't forgive, it eats away at us, causing hate, resentment and regret. We go diving into self-pity and live the rest of our lives as victims of other people's harm. It's a real spiritual and emotional release to 'forgive those who trespass against us.'

"I think about the consequences of their actions on themselves, family, workmates, friends and the community. Just because they are cops, they think they can outsmart their fellow cops and not get caught. They also think that criminals outside will turn on each other, but never corrupt cops. How wrong they were. It was one of their own they turned the tables and went against them to 'dob' them in. They don't realise that the cops from Internal

Affairs used the same investigative methods to catch them as they used to catch criminals. It's like the designer of a 'bear trap' getting caught in his own trap.

"The Internal Affair's police were always a step ahead of the corrupt police, however the corrupt police thought it was the other way around. What a shock they had when they were caught 'red-handed' by recorded audio, video pictures, still photos and undercover police evidence. Even the drug dealers turned on them and gave evidence. They were like rabbits in the middle of a road being startled by a vehicle's bright headlights. They were immobilised and squashed in a second by the same law they had sworn to uphold.

"At the same time, this must be said: the Manly Police Station was understaffed. No department suffered more than the detectives. Some crimes were never investigated. People were told the matter was in hand; the favourite comment was, "We'll investigate the crime when we get to it, we prioritise". That meant it was placed in a pile. A file that was to be opened when more detectives were available. People retired or were transferred but were not replaced."

Supervision was not all it could be. Two detectives were close to retirement and as would be expected, their pace had slackened. There were a limited number of designated (qualified) detectives so Gary had to place two uniformed officers in the role of plain clothes police to help the situation.

Pressure was applied when Gary was directed by the Region Commander to catch up on outstanding 'Operation Noah' files at Manly. 'Operation Noah' was conducted once a year or so when members of the community would ring anonymously with drug crime information for police to follow up. Gary directed the detectives to work on these files. Little did Gary know, this played right into the hands of the corrupt police. Like 'kids loose in a lolly shop'.

Peattie, who'd been a good police officer in the past, aided and abetted Dave Patison, Matthew Jasper, Shaun Davidson,

Mark Messenger and David Hill in their criminal enterprises. It was so sad, after a quarter of a century of policing. To think he threw it away for a pittance. Peattie only got the dregs, the crumbs from the rich man's table—drinking money, whereas Patison and Jasper took the cream of the money without telling him. No honour among thieves, even thieving cops.

This matter of corruption at Manly went on not just a few weeks or a few months but years passed before the axe fell on the unsuspecting band of rogues who were operating inside the police force. Around about 1999 evidence emerged from a police informant (whose name was kept under wraps) that some of the Manly and Dee Why detectives were corrupt. Nothing filtered through to Commander Raymond. Even after some police were stopped in their tracks, there was no way by which Raymond was able to obtain an explanation from Commissioner Ryan. One wonders how times and people can change situations.

At no time before, during or after Operation Florida did Commissioner Ryan make contact with Gary. Gary says, "At no time did Mr. Ryan say anything to me about the corruption. Looking back, I wonder why the Commissioner of Police would allow the corruption to continue for so long. I believe the police informant went straight to him, the Police Integrity Commission or the State Crime Commission. The corruption continued for a long time even until the end of 2000 before the offenders were arrested."

It was this slow response that frightened Gary as he pondered the while situation at the time and ever since.

Gary further says, "That's the thing I found strange and scary. Ryan allowed armed police officers and some armed drug dealers to continue their criminal activities without being apprehended. I can only believe he let the matter go on in order to see how many were involved and how widespread the corruption was. That's the thing I find strange looking back. Not only were these two groups on different sides of the law but also there was a great danger in allowing then matter to drag on for so long. War could have erupted between the corrupt cops and the drug dealers at any time and place over greed and control. Not only were the innocent members of the community at risk, but also the families of corrupt detectives were in danger of violence like drive by shootings or arson."

Gary continues, "My question then and now is why did Commissioner Ryan allow such a dangerous situation go on as long as he did? Another moral and lawful dilemma arises. All this time, illegal drugs were being sold to people (including kids) on the street with full knowledge of the corrupt police and the various police corruption fighting bodies. Not that the drug users couldn't get drugs from other sources, but under Operation Florida it was a free for all. We will never know the human toll inflicted during this 'fishing trip' for police corruption going on for so long.

"It would have only taken two or three weeks to find the extent of the corruption network. Not only drug dealing itself; what about the other issues of corruption? Offenders were not being arrested for crimes, prosecutions failed, justice perverted, police time misused and public money wasted. In fact, it would be impossible to trace where the heroin and marijuana went that was part of the corruption. I believe that by leaving drugs on the street for so long, Ryan failed the community miserably."

Gary is still puzzled about the way Ryan excluded him from his confidence during the Manly corruption, since there was no reason for the exclusion except that Gary may well have been able to stop it.

Gary explains, "It's like a Commander of a naval fleet that sees one of his ships heading towards an iceberg and doesn't tell the Captain or the navigator but allows the ship to plough full steam into the ice just 'to see what would happen'. Like an experiment. You'd think some explanation would be forthcoming, even if it couldn't be given at the time. Letting this operation go on for so long is akin to the police watching a gang of robbers continue to rob just to gather intelligence. It's unnecessary. From the start, they knew who the corrupt cops were due to the information from the police whistle blower. By keeping the corruption to himself, did Ryan try to big note himself or was he afraid of Gary Raymond's probable intervention to stop the corruption? Evidently, 'bud nipping' was not on Ryan's agenda."

When all has been said and done, there was not a skerrick of evidence Raymond was corrupt. A matter of fact, Ryan should have known Gary was a Qualified Senior Internal Affairs Investigator and was deeply trusted.

On one occasion, a man anonymously rang Gary at his office and said the police were at his place to execute a search warrant and he was up the road watching. The man said he might be loaded up by the police. He told Gary he had rang some police from Internal Affairs and they told him that police were not lawfully allowed to execute a Search Warrant without him being present at his home. Gary informed the man this was not true. Police can execute a search warrant if the owner or occupier of the premises is absent. They might be interstate or even overseas and police need to strike 'while the iron's hot.'

Gary knew the man was having him on as no police (especially Internal Affairs) would have given him that misleading advice. Gary also informed the man that the search would be recorded by video camera with an independent police officer present. Gary told the man to go down to his house and be present for the search. The man hung up the phone. Gary heard no more until the PIC enquiry when the phone call was played back. It had been recorded as all the phones in the Manly Command had been tapped on a warrant. Gary still doesn't know to this day whether the phone call was a set up or genuine. PIC interpreted Gary's response to the call as a floor in management. Gary denied this assumption and still believes the man on the phone misled him with false information. To put it straight, he lied.

Ryan knew Gary was a committed Christian. There is no way in the world Ryan would have placed Gary in the position of Commander at Manly Police Station if he'd smelt the slightest sniff of corruption around him. Ryan knew of Gary's exemplary record. He knew he was an enthusiastic crime fighter and a strong leader of police. Further, in his entire career there had not been the slightest indications of anything corrupt. Simply put, he was led as a lamb to the slaughter by Ryan, a trophy on Ryan's mantelpiece.

The Integrity Commission report noted regarding Gary Raymond, "There is no evidence Raymond was implicated in, or knew of, the corrupt activity that took place in his command. His explanation for the ability of the officers to act corruptly was that…. their extremely sneaky and deceiving practices eluded any detection by me or my staff and that he did not think that people would engage in that sort of behaviour, particularly after the Wood Royal Commission."

Gary's corrupt police were experts who knew all the tricks of the trade. They say 'where there's smoke there's fire' but in his command, Gary didn't even smell or see any smoke, otherwise he would have 'extinguished' the fire.

As Gary reported to the Commission enquiry: "…I had no red flags that the procedures weren't being followed and I had the monthly reports saying that they were being followed, so I didn't suspect for one minute that they weren't following the standard operating procedures."

As would be expected, there were some criticisms of Raymond's handling of the situation. Yet it's easy in hindsight to say what he could have done. Hindsight is a wonderful thing to spread around.

In spite of criticism of Gary's handling of the situation at Manly, the Integrity Commission did concede: "There is some force in Raymond's argument that because of the extremely clever and deceitful mode of operation of the corrupt officers, the systems available were not capable of detecting their corrupt conduct. While Raymond put in place the conventional strategies for the prevention and detection of corruption, the lesson seems to be that it is necessary to take further steps than the mere establishment of those structures, to ensure that they are effective."

Such statements flow with ease when one looks backward. After all Raymond in the circumstances considered he had in place appropriate anti-corruption strategies. This being the case, why wouldn't he be satisfied?

Of the corruption at Manly, Gary says, "Corruption brings a neglect of duty. There develops a looking for opportunities as the offender asks, 'What's in it for me'? And so the corrupt police continued their activities. Because they were not stopped, the double-dealing went on with greater risks. More drugs changed hands, more money changed hands. Crime breeds crime and these corrupt cops were looking for top dollar."

There was no logical reason in the world to allow the corrupt cops to go on their merry way. They could have been nipped in the bud, halted at the cross road of their double deals. The fact is they could have been arrested early. In fact, in the first couple of months.

According to Gary, "During all this time the corrupt detectives were loading offenders with minor things they had not done. The reason for calling it a day in the early stages was that the inside informer had provided the names required of those involved, not only the first informer, but others who were subsequently added as whistle blowers. They could have called a halt in the early stages. They let them run. They filmed them, followed them with surveillance cameras. They took photos arranged phone taps. What more was required?

"They let them go so long and the number of offences continued. There was enough evidence to arrest the offenders, charge them, convict and jail them and have them out of the police force. Allowing these corrupt police to continue having a ball meant a longer more expensive and costly Police Integrity Commission hearing. But that was not the end of the story. There was the cost of court proceedings was tremendous and all added to the public purse. Patison and Jasper got 7 years, certainly a significant number of years in jail for former police officers. During 'Operation Florida' the drug dealers were getting angry with the police who were getting the larger share of the profits. They were ripping off too much, getting greedy. The mere fact that Patison and company were taking too much in their 'deals' meant they placed their non-corrupt workmates at risk. At any moment one or other of the drug dealers could have turned violent. I look back on these events with a great deal of disappointment and fear. I can only be thankful to God nothing went wrong leading to death or serious injury. I shudder to think of what might have happened."

Asked about how Parison and Jasper got away with their dealings this answer came back from Gary: "They were amiable, almost too friendly. This meant there were no complaints from the crooks. Nobody said, 'We've been beaten up'. There were no black eyes or bruises. All were getting a share of the spoils. Maybe it wasn't an exact fair share, but it was a share. For whatever reason, the corrupt cops went on their merry way. This whole activity caused the corrupt cops to live on the edge.

"To the best of the knowledge available the serious corruptions carried out by Patison and Jasper started in 1998. Information was soon gathered that could have had them arrested. Since they carried on one cannot even begin to estimate the cost of hospital, ambulance, or doctors required due to the drug activity, not to mention the horrific grief to families and friends of drug users. Then there was the tremendous cost of the investigation, surveillance and court costs. The real cost remains concealed amid the labyrinth of financial estimates.

"Finally, drug dealers were also convicted. All involved could have been charged, convicted and jailed so much earlier if appropriate action had been taken. Peter Ryan allowed these corrupt cops to continue well past their use by date. Did anyone question Ryan or was he beyond reproach? No one knew. When this all came out didn't anyone say, 'Why didn't you act'? Some people asked but got the reply, we wanted to see the extent of the corruption."

On the 13 October 2001, Ryan was reported in speaking to ABCTV, "There will always be failings. You could bring a saint in here and there would be failings. But I'm on the job, I'm doing the job, I'm chasing corrupt police down, (the public) can have every confidence I'm doing it."

Did Ryan's reference to 'sainthood' excuse his failing of not informing his Commander at Manly regarding what was happening under his very feet?

The Wikipedia encyclopaedia website tells us:

"Soon after the 2000 Sydney Olympics Ryan was to quit his post as Commissioner of Police on acrimonious terms. He has since lived in countries like Greece, Doha and Dubai focusing on security consultancy work and working on various international events such as the 2004 Athens Olympics, 2006 Winter Olympics in Turin and the 2008 Beijing Olympics."

The sad thing was that Peattie would allow Patterson, Jasper or Messenger to operate, as they liked. Proceeding to a place, they would discover money, leave it in the drawer where they found it, then take an offender to the police station where he'd be charged on a minor offence. When they returned to the house, they would open the drawer with the money and split it. They then gave the offender say a third and keep two thirds themselves.

Sometimes Patison and Jasper would stuff an amount of cash down the trousers. Larger amounts meant they'd return later to collect. These larger amounts could be many thousands of dollars. A key strategy in tracking down the corrupt police, was 'integrity testing.' Integrity testing of corrupt officers was recommended by the Royal Commission into the New South Wales Police Service in its report of May 1997. This allowed for the testing of the honesty of suspect police officers. Such tests revealed that certain police officers were open to being bribed.

Gary, who was accused of being naive as a Commander says, "There was no evidence my staff were not doing their job. The other thing is, some of the officers like Hill, who had some corruption in the past, had gone straight. But he was set up when an undercover police officer offered him money and he took it. This was an integrity test. Wasn't this entrapment? No, he was sorely tempted. When tempted, he reverted to the past. There is a difference for he'd done this before. Mind you, Hill was called the 'King of the Kids'. He loved being admired by younger police officers. He was anti-authority. He required a lot of approval and ego building.

"I think his taking bribes were an act of defiance against authority as well as for personal gain. He had an elevated sense of justice. He often approached me and spoke against what he thought was an injustice, but he didn't have an elevated sense of justice in his own life. Sadly, there were those who would not normally have taken bribes. But they failed the integrity test, whereas Patison, Jasper Peattie and Messenger (from the Northern Beaches Command) just made it a lifestyle."

To further make it clear, Gary Raymond was no fool and well prepared to deal with corruption. When he was at Cabramatta it was brought to his notice that a certain police officer was corrupt. He had that officer charged with 'Goods in Custody' after a theft in premises that had been broken into by a criminal. At Manly he sacked an officer using illegal drugs.

Regarding Ray Peattie, Gary said, "Why wouldn't you trust your second in command? There was not the slightest indication otherwise. Because of this you would automatically trust your second in command. Peattie performed well. He was doing what I asked. We got on well. He had achievable results. He was causing a reduction in crime due to tactical operations. These guys were clever. They constantly put drugs and cash in the exhibits. Who could tell they were skimming off the top? To make matters a little amusing, I even received a commendation from one of the Region Commanders for our effective drug seizures."

These corrupt police covered themselves by appearing to do real police work. What amazed Gary was how these cops could be corrupt one day and literally protect the community from an axe-wielding offender the next.

Gary says, "For example let me explain how crafty they were. My number two in charge of Manly Police Station, my Crime Manager Ray Peattie was corrupt beyond belief. You don't get much through to you when your second in command is a bad egg. The corrupt police would choose Peattie as the independent officer for a search warrant. The independent officer goes along as a watchdog. He's supposed to make sure the video camera is recording.

"However, Patison would stand in the way with his back to Peattie or Peattie would go outside for a smoke. Either way Peattie aided and abetted the dishonest police. They would choose him instead of a non-corrupt duty officer. Peattie would seize the opportunity and quickly volunteer to attend a search warrant. I thought he was saving the duty officer time allowing him to perform other tasks. I also thought he was keen because he had the Command at heart."

Matters started to unravel on the morning of Thursday 4 October 2000, when Gary was summoned to Police Headquarters in Sydney. In the foyer before the meeting, Gary met a police psychologist he knew. Gary knew her father who was a serving police officer and used to work with Gary at Redfern Police Station when he first entered the job.

She said, "Hi Gary. What are you doing here?"

"I've got to see Deputy Commissioner Moroney at 12.30. What about you?"

"I've got to be here because a police officer is going to receive bad news in Mr. Moroney's office and they may need counselling and support if they get upset."

Gary paused and so did she. It all twigged.

Gary replied, "Well guess what, that's me you're here to help."

She got really upset and said, "I don't know if I can do this. What is the bad news they're going to give you? Have you any idea?"

Gary said without emotion, "Yes there's been corrupt police

exposed at Manly and Dee Why Commands. I think they're gong to blame me for not picking it up. Come on, we'll do this together. Don't be upset, it's part of the way the system operates, whether we like it or not, or agree with it or not. There has to be a fall guy and it's usually the boss at the time. That's me. Like the Titanic. Blame the Captain for what the crew did or didn't do even though he was in bed at the time. I can assure you, if I found evidence of corruption I would have come down on them 'like a ton of bricks' and had them arrested. There was no signs; they were very clever."

Gary walked into Deputy Commissioner Moroney's office and took a seat. Gary heard a noise behind him. A man appeared from behind the door (yes, behind the door) and said, "Gary Raymond, I have a summons for you to appear before the Police Integrity Commission (PIC)."

Moroney said, "I'm sorry, you'll have to be taken out of your Command, Gary. You will work out of Region Headquarters at Gosford for the time being."

Gary didn't reply, shook hands with Moroney and left with his summons. The police psychologist left with Gary, extremely upset. Gary was calm and understood that the system was like a huge monster that could not be stopped. He knew he had no choice but to get chewed up and spat out by the procedures surrounding him. Gary had a deep trust that God had a plan in all of this mayhem and that God knew the summons was coming, putting Gary right into the middle of it for a greater purpose.

On Friday 5 October 2001, Gary was removed from the command of the Manly-Davidson Local Area Police. Commissioner Peter Ryan's statement said, "Raymond had been removed for the duration of the Police Integrity Commission Enquiry."

From the time the corruption was openly revealed, Gary was certainly in the firing line and had allegations of mismanagement placed at his feet because he didn't discover the corruption at Manly. The corrupt officer Mark Messenger, at the Northern

Beaches Command, wasn't discovered by the Local Area Commander there either. No regress there.

They were ill informed and did not understand that this was standard procedure in such situations to relieve a Commander from operational responsibility, enabling him/her to attend the Commission hearings each day and give evidence. Unfortunately, when the media heard that Gary had been asked to 'stand aside' some newspapers and a TV channel reported that he had been stood down, suspended or sacked. This is a form of sensationalism, which sells news. Alan Jones on 2GB radio was the worst.

Gary just couldn't believe his eyes when TV stations were running undercover surveillance video pictures of the corrupt cops getting bribes in stairwells and public parks before the footage was even entered into evidence at PIC. Can you imagine splashing evidence to the media before a trial? They would drag you over the coals and prefer charges in court.

Who gave permission to release the footage?

Who gave the media that footage?

Why was it shown before any proceedings?

Why weren't people brought to account for releasing (or leaking) the evidence?

Will we ever know?

Gary had to go to Police Region Headquarters at Gosford, which was an hour and half north from his home in Sydney. Gary's police car was taken off him. He was no longer Commander of Manly. His car was left at Police Headquarters in Sydney. Gary tried to get involved at Gosford Region. The Regional Commander had meetings with his local commanders, but Gary was not included. Fellow commanders were very supportive, however his removal from Manly was a blow to his pride and tremendous hit against all he had stood for regarding trust.

He'd trusted his fellow police and had been sadly let down. However, the one thing that kept Gary safe and sane in the situation was his Christian faith. As a strong believer in Christ and in the Bible his faith made him stand firm in spite of the swirling accusations around him. After a while, Gary gained an understanding that God was present with him in all of this. Gary became bored with doing nothing and asked for meaningful work whilst waiting for the PIC enquiry.

Subsequently, Gary was posted to Parramatta to work with Assistant Commissioner Chris Evans as a Terrorism Risk Assessor, working on the security and safety of the upcoming Rugby World Cup in 2003. They had to consider the prevention and police response in case of terrorism. He really enjoyed this work and being under the command of Chris Evans was a bonus. Chris helped build up Gary's self esteem. During this time Gary and the team authored a comprehensive Terrorism Risk Assessment, which even to this day is used by other law enforcement agencies as a model of best practice.

After the Rugby World Cup, Gary was sent to Blacktown to work alongside Superintendent Les Wales, the Local Area Commander. He was to assist Les, with Les in turn passing on leadership skills. It was like putting two captains on the bridge of the same ship. Gary was reluctant to make decisions or initiate changes. He could not exercise his command in another Superintendent's jurisdiction. It was a waste of Gary's and Les's time. Anyway, there were shadows over Gary's head until the commission brought down its findings. The findings eventually totally exonerated Gary.

There were those in the job at the time who advised Gary that he had the opportunity to get out on Hurt On Duty (HOD) stress leave and get a healthy pension, if he wanted to. Gary immediately dismissed this as morally wrong and continued through God's strength and grace. Gary was not stressed to the point of leaving the cops, so why put on a farce that he was for the money?

So came to a close one of the saddest periods in the life of the New South Wales Police. The report stated the 46 year old Peattie, father of three, and his fellow corrupt police stood ashen faced before the judge. One could only surmise the troubled heart of these men. There was a total of 78 days of public hearings. In addition, the investigation included a number of private hearings, the last day the private hearings being 27 August 2003. There were a total of 99 witnesses who gave evidence, 95 in public hearings and 4 in private hearings. The evidence, which was later released in public proceedings. Of the 99 witnesses, 32 were serving New South Wales police officers at the time they gave evidence, 31 were former officers and 36 were civilians. 14 of the 32 serving officers left the New South Wales Police Force, 11 of those as a direct result of the investigation.

Most important for the purpose of this book, the following was recorded by the Police Integrity Commission regarding Gary Raymond:

"The Report drew attention to the difficulty of the Commander's office being geographically separate from the police station at which the operational police worked. ...Because of the extremely clever and deceitful mode of operation of the corrupt officers, the systems available were not capable of detecting their corrupt conduct. While Commander Raymond put in place the conventional strategies for the prevention and detection of corruption, the lesson seems to be that it is necessary to take further steps than the mere establishment of those structures to ensure that they are relative."

On 5 January 2001, Ian Ball, President of the New South Wales Police Association wrote these words to encourage members of the force:

"I understand there have been some allegations about a relatively small number of people who have allegedly been misbehaving in regard to drug issues. Naturally, there is a need for due process however the honest cops of New South Wales reject absolutely anyone engaging in criminal conduct, especially involving drugs. "The PANSW (Police Association of New South Wales) is still cleaning up what some described as collateral damage from the Royal Commission and so, we as a membership do not accept that any innocent police officer should ever be treated as collateral damage.

"There are hundreds of processional, honest and devoted police officers attached to the Local Area Commands apparently under examination. All those police deserve our wholehearted support and I trust that we can all, in some way, let them know that we are all thinking of them. We support the activities of the Police Integrity Commission in getting rid of any person engaged in this sort of misbehaviour. Equally, we seek that government, media and the community understand and support the many thousands of honest police officers going about their duty in their normal professional manner.

"I have always been proud to be a cop. I still am and I just hope that the thousands of honest cops in this state keep their chins up and go on doing their duty. Don't worry about the rubbish that some will throw at us. Keep locking up crooks and helping victims. That's what being in the cops is all about."

Part Two: Coming to Terms

The Sydney *Daily Telegraph* in December 2001 reported,

"Manly local area commander Gary Raymond told the Police Integrity Commission corrupt detectives under him were using 'sneaky and deceiving practices' of which he was unaware." The report also reported Gary as saying, "Looking back, the corrupt officers were the most experienced…had they been honest they would have done a very good job."

Because of the criminal activities of a corrupt few, their network took huge sums of money, even amounts of $50,000. The half will never be told. The outcome of the investigations conducted by 'Operation Florida' proved Gary had not been implicated in the network of crime by those devious detectives under him. Neither was there any implication of corruption carried out by Gary. The Police Commissioner and the Queen's Council assisting the Police Integrity Commissioner exonerated him for he and many others at the Manly Police Station did not have knowledge of any corrupt activities or even the undercover

TANGLED WAYS

Police that finally exposed the corruption.

Gary told me, "Regarding staff relations, I had good rapport with them. As for the area itself it was called the 'Insular Peninsular'. Many of the staff at Manly Police Station had lived in the area for many years with their surfing, football, school or university friends. They had been to each other's weddings, shared in social events and holidays. Remarkably, some had never ever been to Sydney's western suburbs in their life. They were socially knitted together and committed to the Manly area because they had everything they needed over there: nice beaches, good recreation facilities such as clubs, parks, shops, business premises. There was no need to go anywhere else.

"Many of the staff had never seen Blacktown or Mt Druitt. They had driven through on the way to the Blue Mountains. At one stage, I talked to them about maybe an exchange with other police stations to do a short shift there for 'experience sake'. The idea did not get off the ground. They had no desire to step foot in the west or spend anytime policing it. As for the Manly shopping precinct, it was a vibrant area. We had at least 90 licensed premises. This meant there was often an alcohol problem with drunkenness among backpackers."

Part Three: Power to Forgive

I asked Gary how he responded after he found out his second in command was crooked to the core. His response: "One day without warning, the Police Integrity Commission and Police Internal Affairs Investigation Unit raided The Manly Police Station with search warrants in hand. This was one of the greatest shocks of my life. I asked what it was all about. I was told we were being investigated. A number of staff were corrupt. The crooked cops were headed up by my second in command.

"The Acting Detective Inspector's false front came as a total surprise. I wondered how could a person be that secretive? The Bible says that all of us have fallen short of God's glorious ideal (Romans 3:23). How can one tell just by looking and speaking to somebody what secret sin lies well below the surface? I couldn't believe that police officers who upheld such high ideals could turn into such low criminals.

"I felt betrayed and angry at such a betrayal. I felt sorry for him and his family knowing that he was going to suffer and his family and workmates would be left to pick up the pieces. As the publicity came out, the PIC evidence was shown on television by way of hidden cameras. The extent of the corruption and the way in which it was concealed was a revelation to the entire New South Wales Police Force and community. The Detective Inspector and a number of other corrupt police were charged with criminal offences. I was jolted back to where the Bible says how we can be forgiven, if we do not forgive others? (Colossians 3:13)

"With that, I wept and thanked God for the forgiveness he offers all of us. Weeks later, I saw the suspended Detective Inspector and with tears in his eyes, he said he was sorry to have brought all the shame on the police force, me and my wife Michelle. I told him that if he repented, put his faith and trust in Christ, God would see him through this. I then prayed with him, He wept more deeply. To my knowledge he is not 'born again' yet, but he will be.

"It's worth noting that if police officers are put in jail, they will get bashed up, so they are put in a special facility, such as Cooma Jail. The simple fact is they would not survive if placed in a normal jail situation, for they would be constantly under threat of being assaulted or even murdered. Therefore, they're placed in a special situation for their own protection. When a police officer gets bent, there is not much sympathy found for him among criminals, serving police or the general community. In a similar way, criminals such as the Cobby killers had to be separated.

"There's a strange and somewhat perverted philosophy among criminals. You can rape and kill anyone except those in the in the caring or religious professions. Doctors, nurses, ambulance officers, Salvation Army officers or nuns. Neither do you dare touch children. This is why paedophiles present a problem in jail.

TANGLED WAYS

Placing them in protection is quite a headache for the authorities. In the case of Anita Cobby's killers, there was a clear distinction between other assaults and the assault of a nurse. For this reason each of the five men involved in the Cobby killing have had to watch their backs in jail, and will do so for the rest of their lives, for they have been marked never to be released. In the case of John Travers, the leader in this horrific event, he is often in solitary confinement."

In reviewing the 'Florida Affair' Gary, rather than being critical of Commissioner Peter Ryan, is puzzled by the handling of the matter. On the other hand, the puzzlement could have been avoided by a simple word. Then again, maybe there were some unknown factors which prevented the truth coming out. Gary continues to ponder and wonder why. Why was he made a scapegoat? Then again, there are mysteries within all of us that will not be revealed this side of heaven. Finally, we must surely recognise it's wisest never to predict people for even the worst of us and the best of us are unpredictable. In summing up the 'Florida Affair' let's say this one rule holds good - 'NEVER PREDICT PEOPLE.'

When Gary retired in December 2005, he received the following letter from Police Commissioner Ken Moroney:

Dear Gary,

I thought it opportune that I should write to you on this very special occasion, namely, your retirement from the New South Wales Police. I am sure that this is a time to reflect on all that you have achieved throughout a lifetime of distinguished service and commitment to the people of New South Wales and for us to acknowledge your service and commitment with thanks and appreciation. In so many ways then, thank you seems inadequate and perhaps trite, but nevertheless, you should know that with our appreciation and admiration for you as a fellow Police Officer goes our sincere thanks for a job well done.

In every way, you have been true to your Oath of Office –

an oath taken so long ago on the parade ground at the Police Academy, Redfern. By any measure, you epitomise your sacred oath in that you have always done your job to the very best of your skill and ability. No more was asked of you and most assuredly in your case no less was ever given. In many ways, you are not lost to the organization. Whilst you now move on to the next stage of your life and begin a new career, your courage and selflessness (together with so many others) will be forevermore epitomised by a fateful day at Granville.

Someone has told me that 'Day of the Roses' is to be remade into a full length movie and that you have asked Pierce Brosnan to play you. Could that be so? Finally my friend, all that you have achieved both personally and professionally, is, as I am sure you are well aware, achieved by the love and support of your family. We could not and would not do the job that is required of us without that love and support. Now it is time for us to return you to the family perhaps a little older, a little greyer but hopefully still in working order. Our appreciation extends to your wife and family for their invaluable support to you and us. Thank you for the job you have done. Thank you also for your friendship, your camaraderie, your leadership and above all else, thanks for just being you. You have actively contributed to the proud traditions and history that is the New South Wales Police and in doing so you have earned well deserved retirement.

Every best wish for the future,

Yours sincerely,
K.E. MORONEY AO, APM, MA.

CHAPTER FOUR

TIME FOR TEARS

"Tears shed for self are tears of weakness, but shed for others are a sign of strength." *Billy Graham*

Wheelchair Incident

Gary has a friend who used to lead a Bible study. The friend moved away but came back with his wife to visit Gary and Michelle. Gary and Michelle decided to take the friend and his wife into Darling Harbour for a nice meal. Returning home along Parramatta Road, they were near Annandale. On their right, on the footpath, they saw a large group of drunken men skylarking, yelling and falling over each other. It seemed as if it was a 'buck's night' out. This turned out to be right. There was a young man in a wheelchair. He was taking an active part in the larrikinism. Because there was no traffic at the time, the young man wheeled his chair out into the middle of the road and started propelling the chair in circles doing 'doughnuts'. He was acting like an idiot. All his mates cheered, clapped, laughed, and egged him on.

At this point, unbeknown to the man in the wheelchair, the traffic started to pour down the hill towards him. The man tried to get back over the medium strip to the other side of the road but couldn't get up the strip with his front wheels. The chair suddenly tipped over backwards and the man fell onto the roadway right in front of a car. Like a horror movie, the car, no time to brake, ran over his head, which killed him instantly, right in front of

Gary, Michelle and their friends. Other cars came to a screeching halt. All the man's mates screamed and yelled. Some ran away, others ran hysterically onto the road, staring at their dead mate. Traffic was screeching everywhere to avoid the people. One mate, gasping and crying tried, CPR by pressing his chest. It was useless of course, but I suppose he thought he was helping.

Gary parked his car and went to the scene, announcing he was a police officer. He carefully led the man who was doing CPR away from the body, assuring him he had done his best for his mate. Gary looked around at the scene and began to take charge. He asked if anyone had a blanket or tarp in their car. A man gave Gary a blanket, with which he covered the man's body and surrounding area to preserve evidence and prevent more people seeing the grotesque sight. Gary put traffic diversions in place and used rope to cordon off the scene. Gary had to continue his role until other on duty police arrived. Triple '0' was dialled and an ambulance soon arrived at the scene. Some of the man's mates were hysterical in disbelief. Some were out of control. Some cried, cuddled each other screaming, some kicked lamp posts. They were certainly in serious denial as well. Seven or eight minutes later, a police car arrived.

Gary thought he could hand over to the constables who got out of the car, however they had never handled a fatal incident before. Gary continued his role until a Supervising Sergeant arrived. Gary later did a statement for the Coroner. For Gary, his wife and their friends, it was a very tragic end to what had been a pleasant night out at Darling Harbour. The memory of the man in the wheelchair will stay long in their memories.

Gary said, "When you attend a critical incident, the sensory stimuli like sights, sounds, smells and touches may give you flashbacks or dreams long after the incident. You may also see, hear, smell or touch things that remind you of the incident well into the future. It's all a normal response to an abnormal event." One thing it reminded Gary of was the tragic consequences of alcohol-fuelled, so-called fun, and the peer pressure to show off to get the approval from an admiring and misguided crowd.

Drop the Bottle.
One night Gary was on the Christian street team in the early hours of the morning. The kebab shop at Blacktown reported that an Aboriginal youth was drunk and disorderly. He was drinking a bottle of beer and yelling abuse at the world at large. Suddenly, he held it by the stem and smashed it hard on the gutter. Gary told people to stay away, for it looked as if the youth might attack people. Gary could not understand what the youth was saying as he muttered away to himself. Without warning, the youth slashed his left wrist then his right with the sharp edges of the bottle. Blood spurted up in the air from both wrists. Street kids who were watching screamed.

Team members and street kids wanted to rush in and help but by now, the youth was running around in circles holding the broken and blood stained bottle up to his throat, threatening to cut it. The blood was going everywhere, with the youth's face turning red. Gary became assertive and told everyone to stay away from the bleeding youth. He held his arms out keeping people back. Gary repeatedly yelled, "Drop the bottle mate, and drop it now." Gary was not going to approach the youth still armed with the bottle. He might purposely attack Gary or slash himself again, and if Gary was in the way, inadvertently slice or stab him.

A number of the street kids yelled frantically, "Mr Raymond, he's bleeding to death, please help him, he's going to bleed to death. Mr Raymond, do something." The male kids were angry and the females crying. Gary told them to stay back and that the youth would not bleed to death and that he was waiting for him to give up the bottle before helping him with first aid. Gary realised that non police officers would not understand the risks in this situation.

Moments later, the youth threw the bottle away and sat in the gutter with blood still spurting from his wrists. Gary again told everyone to stay away. He put on surgical gloves, which they always carried on street team. Gary carefully approached the youth from behind whilst asking him whether he carried another weapon, like a knife. Gary did a quick pat-down search which was clear. He then went the side of the youth, grabbed both wrists and inserted direct pressure onto the ends of the bleeding arteries. The youth protested and begged Gary to let him die. He tried to pull away but Gary held him down as he continued to sit in the gutter.

Gary sat in front of him still holding the youth's wrists. A crowd gathered around. The police and ambulance had been called and Gary could hear sirens in the background. When the youth heard the sirens, he became distressed, cried and tried to stand up. Gary gently restrained the weakened youth and reassured him he would be okay. The bleeding was now down to an ooze from the wounds. Gary continued to hold on pressure and elevated both wrists. Gary estimated the youth had lost a litre of blood, which is serious. Gary asked the youth to lie on his back on the footpath, which he did. Gary told one of the street team to raise the youth's legs and hold them in an effort to treat for shock. As the youth cried, Gary felt an enormous compassion for him. Gary wondered what had led to this drastic action and what events in his life had brought him down.

Gary said, "The alcohol didn't help his depression. People with problems shouldn't get drunk or take non-prescribed drugs as it leads them to disregard their own safety and security. They lose all sense of reason and begin to do irrational things. Even if they don't deliberately do something harmful, they may accidently hurt themselves. They are particularly vulnerable to pedestrian collision on roads or railways, tripping, slipping or falling from heights, not to mention life threatening medical conditions. Serious head injuries are common. These people are also at risk as victims of assault, robbery, rape or theft."

As Gary's heart broke for this young man, he began to gently pray with him. He asked God to show this young man what Jesus did on the cross for him by dying and rising from the dead; that

TIME FOR TEARS

God would show him He had a good plan for his life. The sirens switched off as the police and ambulance arrived. Gary briefed them and they took over. After the emergency services left to take the youth to hospital, Gary gathered the team and the street kids together and explained to them the actions that he took in the situation and why. Gary dealt with just as many dramas off duty on street team as he did on duty in his police car. Gary told me, "As a Christian you learn to allow God to use you to show His love anywhere, at any time to anyone."

Dad Suicides
Early one evening a call came through to Blacktown Police Station. A man's neighbour heard a loud bang next door, which she thought, might have been a gunshot. The police arrived, checked the house from the outside, gained entry and found the body of a 35 old man slumped on a lounge with a firearm between his legs.

Gary, as Duty Officer, attended the scene. The crime scene was preserved. A Forensic Services team and detectives were called. After the team had finished, Gary had a look around and found a large bag full of firearms, which were subsequently found to be unregistered. The man did not have a firearm licence. The first thought that dawned on Gary was the number of firearms that are out in the community that the authorities don't know about. Gary saw many examples of this when he worked at Cabramatta. The illegal firearms are cheap and readily available, not to mention those that can be homemade or on three-dimensional material printers.

Gary looked around the house and saw toys, equipment and other items that strongly suggested that children probably lived in the house. Gary then asked the police officers present if they had thought to search the house, especially the roof space and under the house?

One said, "Well, we haven't, Sir."

Gary snapped back: "Get it done now. How do you know he

hasn't killed anybody before he suicided? Be careful of booby traps, explosive devices or other hazardous materials."

"Yes, Sir," was the embarrassed reply.

The search revealed no more bodies, but more firearms in the roof space, not far from the manhole. The officers were most apologetic to Gary, who said, "You live and learn. Remember, it's often not what you see, but what you don't see at crime scenes."

It was later discovered that the man and his wife had a turbulent marriage. After a heated argument, she left with their four children to live somewhere else. Just prior to the removal of the body, Gary sadly noticed some of the man's brain matter had splattered onto a photo of his children. Gary became very upset with his thoughts immediately going to the man's children, who would soon suffer the lifelong consequences of their father's suicide.

He thought of the enormous loss and pain they would suffer for their entire lives as the result of their father's act. Gary pondered what their reaction would be when he knocked on their door and gave them the tragic news. As Duty Officer the job fell to him to inform them of his death. He didn't want to do it, but knew he had too.

As Gary stared at the photo on the wall, he was deeply moved. So moved he started to grind his teeth in anger. Even though he knew its well-documented people who suicide are self-centred, unless they're psychotic, in which case they're confused, he knew it's an 'all about me act' and nobody else is usually considered in the planning. People in such a situation become bound by the north, south, east and west of self and their own issues. They become enraptured their own capsule of life. The world becomes their oyster. Others cease to matter anymore, if ever.

In their mind they're doing the world a favour by suiciding when in fact their decisions are devastating others. "Everyone is better off without me," they say, not calculating the cost to those left behind. Some who suicide consider they are doing their loved ones a favour when in fact their loved ones are guttered

TIME FOR TEARS

and left with a lifelong loss.

After a pause, Gary swallowed hard and got his emotions back. He placed on gloves, gently lifting the photo down from the wall. He slowly walked to the kitchen and carefully washed the mess off the glass of the photo. He then carefully placed the photo back on the wall and washed down the wall. He did all this, with the thought in mind, to save the family shock and pain finding the photo in the state in which he found it.

These are the 'little' things police do behind the scenes that no-one ever knows or sees; the favours police do by going out of their way to ease the pain of others. No publicity, just thankless tasks done in secret. Police officers have to enter into places where the rest of us never have to go, to see sights the rest of us never have to see, and experience the horrors of what happens when people fall apart. All the more reason we need to pray for our police officers; pray that they might have the courage and stamina to cope with the ugly scenes their eyes are forced to rest on because of what people have done.

Gary took a big breath, knocked on the door of the dead man's wife's unit and waited anxiously. A lady came to the door with a young child holding her hand.

Gary said, "Hello are you Mrs...?"

She said, "Yes."

"May I come in please?"

Gary entered the well lived in lounge room. There were another three children playing and watching TV. They got excited seeing Gary in uniform and approached him asking questions about his pistol, handcuffs and the rest, as kids do.

The lady said," Is this about my husband?"

Gary said," Yes it is."

"He's dead, isn't he?"

Gary surprised said," I'm afraid he is, I'm sorry."

"We're not. Did he shoot himself?"

"Did you want to speak without the children here?"

"Yes, its okay, they have had to grow up way beyond their

years anyway."

"Tell me what you mean."

"He has been violent towards us for a long time. We left him and he threatened suicide but there was no way were going back. He was a control freak and very cranky. I'm glad he's dead."

She wasn't crying, which surprised Gary. Gary figured she must be extremely traumatised by their relationship and almost relieved he was dead to not grieve straight away. Some deaths, like terminal cancer, give the family relief rather than grief. Was this one of those type of deaths?

Gary said gently, "Yes he shot himself in the head."

She replied without emotion, "I knew he would one day. The final payback."

"I'm so sorry all that happened to you and the kids. Did you report any matters to the police or courts?"

"No. He has guns and I was so scared he'd shoot us or a police officer if I reported it. We have lived in fear, until now."

"Yes, we found all the guns. I'm sorry to bring this up, but we need somebody to identify his body at the city morgue. Who can do that?"

"I'm not doing it. I never wanted to see him again ever. His brother can do it; here is his phone number."

"We'll obtain a statement from you soon, for the Coroner."

Gary stayed for about an hour as the woman poured her heart out. She eventually cried. He enquired if she needed anything practical from the Salvation Army or counselling over her and the children's past traumas. She would let Gary know.

Gary told me, "People must immediately report domestic violence to the police. Whether involved or a witness, ring the police. The situation rarely gets better. It goes from verbal abuse, to physical abuse, false imprisonment and even murder. It can also trigger a murder/suicide. How often do you hear of people killing their family and themselves. Love triangles can also trigger such behaviour." This case was extremely sad for all concerned. Another one in Gary's 'memory bank.'

TIME FOR TEARS

Landslide at Thredbo

The village of Thredbo in New South Wales has been described as being set within the magic of Kosciusko National Park; this is one of Australia's highest Alps and is perched amid some huge mountains. In 1955 a man from Czechoslovakia had a vision for a mountain resort and so Thredbo became a place to ski and enjoy the snowfields of the area. Gary was at home. A call came through to say there'd been a catastrophic landslide at Thredbo in the Snowy Mountains region of New South Wales and he was required to attend with the NSW Volunteer Rescue Association Squad.

The sudden collapse of the 3500 tonnes of earth, which caused two lodges at Thredbo to virtually disappear in one huge landslide, sent shock waves across the country. Quite unexpected the landslide wrecked and destroyed Bimbadeen and Carinya lodges, which were nestled in the supposed shelter of Kosciuszko, Australia's highest mountain. It meant there could be around one hundred people trapped in the massive landslide. It was possible. No one knew. The toll was eventually 18 people dead.

At 11.35pm on 30 July 1997, a 'never to be forgotten' night, the news broke, leaving everybody shocked. News reports simply said there were people trapped and buried. Given the enormity of the situation and its location, they thought there would be fatalities. At first Gary thought," I haven't got any snow shoes or winter gear."

He went straight to Parramatta to hire some snow clothes. At the store, he told them he was going down to Thredbo to help with the landslide. They fitted him out with the clothes needed. When Gary tried to pay, the manager said there was no charge to thank him for going, but just the assurance he would bring the gear back afterwards. Gary went home packed a few things, kissed Michelle good-bye and immediately drove to Thredbo.

When he arrived, Gary booked in at the Control Centre, before heading to the actual landslide area. He stared at the slide. A huge wall of rocks and mud had been gouged out and slipped down the slope. There were just bits of damaged buildings sticking out. Liquid mud. Gary followed the road to Thredbo Village. He noticed there was a great deal of activity. Digging equipment and people everywhere. Not too many people on the slide itself, which wasn't hard to work out. It was far too dangerous, like quicksand. While it could not be seen with the naked eye, the debris rich sludge was slowly on the move downwards. Clearly, it was a danger area and he made sure he stayed well clear of the sludgy material.

When Gary reached the Field Control, he attended a briefing to ensure workers were adequately aware of what was going on. Gary then went to the scene. At that time, only four bodies had been recovered. All of the emergency services were on site. There was equipment to locate bodies; it was at an early stage. Gary turned his mind to welfare issues. People were working at the site day and night with the temperature at minus 9 degrees celcius. It was very cold but thankfully not windy.

Gary realised he need to make sure there was enough support to help people with critical incident stress if it occurred. There may also be physical injuries after dragging and lifting equipment on such a steep site. Gary arranged a barbeque and meals for the rescuers from the Salvation Army Emergency Services (SAES). He and some other blokes got hold of a clean empty 44-gallon drum, cut holes in the sides and bottom then placed it in a safe place. He built a nice big log fire in the drum to warm the cold bodies of volunteers when they came off the site.

This fire went on day after day, night after night. Gary figured out people would come out off the site and straight to the fire, which they did. Like bees to a honey pot. He realised it was important to warm them up and give them a cup of tea or coffee with a meal. It worked well. Chaplains and counsellors were also put near the fire so people under stress who came away from the landslide could talk out their feelings if they wanted to. No compulsion, only if they felt comfortable to talk. Gary also took part in this process.

TIME FOR TEARS

One night, a young fellow from the NSW State Emergency Services (SES) came up to the fire after working on the rescue site. He was on his own. People were doing short shifts. This fellow seemed particularly upset. Gary asked him, "What are you thinking mate?" That's a better approach than asking, "What's wrong?" Gary says, you don't ask if there's anything wrong in such situations. Rather you say, "What are you thinking now?" That means you don't pre-judge someone just on their body language or facial expressions.

The youth said, "We dug into a room and found a dead body. I got upset as the smell was the same smell I smelt when my grandfather died not long ago. His body wasn't found for three days. I was reminded of my grandfather."

Gary told the youth his reaction was quite normal. Coming off the site was wise for it gave him an opportunity to recover. Gary talked to him about flashbacks of smells, sights, sounds and touches which can trigger past memories. After they talked and drunk a nice hot cup of tea, the youth was able to return to the landslide site and continue working to find anyone who might be trapped. He was rested and understood his reactions were normal and permissible. As he said goodbye, Gary said, "I'll see you when you finish the shift." The youth said he felt much better. Gary said, "Do your job. Come back and have another cuppa with me." The youth thanked Gary for helping him and went back on site. Gary says it's not uncommon for emergency people to have moments. On reflecting he said, "We remember moments, not days."

Gary remembers how after the Granville train smash, he travelled down Parramatta Road and it seemed surreal to be back in normal life again after 36 hours at a disaster site. You lose track of time, space and what's happening around you in the rest of the world. He thinks it's like getting out of jail or coming home from a war zone: you have to re-orientate back to normal. Having been in a confined space under the collapsed bridge, with people in the trapped train for some ten hours, you flashback in disbelief to what you have just done.

On his duty at Thredbo, Gary was accommodated at no cost in a $600 a night room in an adjoining lodge. Even though this was no skiing holiday, he thanked God for it and said to Him, "I'm staying here and doing this service for you, Lord." Later Gary said, "God puts us in various places to do things for Him. Some of those places are comfortable, some not." On this occasion it was very comfortable, however on missions in India and Sri Lanka, Gary slept on the floor in 'dung' floor huts. Big difference.

Gary confided in me that he didn't sleep that well at Thredbo. He was afraid that another landslide might happen on the site. Where he was sleeping was just west of the disaster site. Engineers said it was stable, however Gary was unsure given what he saw at the collapse site not far away from his room. Like everything else in Gary's life, just another 'trust in God' moment.

I asked Gary, "Were you there when Stuart Diver was found?"

He replied, "No, I was on the other side of the site performing a counselling task." Gary remembers someone saying they'd found a person underneath the rubble. Gary thought, "Wow, how could anyone last in that cold mess for so long. They certainly needed to be tough or shortly die. It was a great rescue effort to get him out 26 hours after being trapped. Sadly, his wife Sally drowned beside him, well before rescue found them." Stuart is a Ski Instructor at Thredbo today. He is now married to Rosanna and has a daughter, Alessia.

I asked what happens in such a situation regarding bodies. Gary said, "You normally have to have Disaster Victim Identification (DVI) police. In the case of Thredbo, bodies were transferred to Sydney because there were far more facilities down there for autopsies. In addition, they have people who can help counsel the relatives. Social workers are here to help. To view or not to view bodies is also a big struggle for some relatives. There are people to advise regarding organ donation as well, if that's a possibility."

Gary told a touching story about his time at Thredbo. An elderly grey haired lady came up to him and asked, "Mr Raymond

TIME FOR TEARS

is anyone washing and ironing your clothing?"

"No", he said.

"I like to do it for you. I can't rescue people but I can do that for you."

He found out she was a lovely Christian lady and God had laid it on her heart to wash clothes for the rescue workers. Gary wanted to pay her, but she said no. When she returned his clothes, he said, "You've even ironed these, haven't you?"

"Yes underpants and singlets."

"Why do you do that?"

"I'm washing and ironing for Jesus. I'm doing it all for Jesus, not you. He's given you the strength on this dreadful disaster and this is the least I can do to help."

When Gary got back home, Michelle commented on the ironed underpants. She said jokingly to Gary, "Don't expect me to iron your underpants, and if I did, I'd do it whilst you were wearing them."

……..Ouch!!

She is normally kind to Gary but as he wisely pointed out, "Don't tangle with a woman with a hot iron in her hand."

The comment by the elderly lady stuck in Gary's mind even to this day: "I'll do it all for Jesus."

Regarding the landslide at Thredbo, Gary says, "Thredbo should never have happened. It was preventable, like all man-made disasters. People underestimate the power of water. The danger lurks unseen. At Thredbo, the risk of water building up on top of the slope before the landslide was not calculated. The road above was not drained correctly. People see the power of water but do not prepare as it builds up over time then suddenly gives away.

"Efficient plumbing would have stopped the slip and avoided all those deaths and property damage. Much of what happens could be avoided. People continue to build in dangerous places, or neglect by people make places dangerous. There's no such thing as an accident."

Gary is often reminded of a Sergeant who used to say, "There's no such thing as an accident, it's an act or an omission by somebody."

Gary also observed, God often gets the blame for human lack of care. People angrily protest, "Where was God when the land slipped"? No, God has given mankind the intelligence and skills to prevent land slips. So who is really to blame?"

A Detective Cries

A detective under Gary had a brother who overdosed on drugs and died. Gary was at home when he received a phone call from a woman who said one of Gary's young detectives was sitting in a gutter crying. Gary was asked to check the matter. He went round to the detective's house and found him sitting outside in the gutter. Gary got out of the car and sat down in the gutter beside the detective. Gary said nothing. There was a fair bit of activity in the house behind the two as they sat there.

Finally, the detective spoke, "Gaz, you don't know about my younger brother. I was ashamed and embarrassed to tell you he was a serious drug addict. Here I am a detective chasing drug dealers and there's my own brother, a raging heroin addict. I've been living with this for years. I've never been game to tell anyone at work." He began to cry. Gary put his arm around his young mate's shoulder.

It then crossed Gary's mind, he'd done drug raids in drug premises and this detective had been particularly hard on drug dealers. On one occasion, Gary had actually pulled him away from a dealer before it got physical. Gary had counselled the detective about his anger management and being very hard on the druggies. There were other times, the same detective had pleaded with Gary to let a drug user go and 'give him a break' instead of arrest.

The young detective was suggesting they use their discretion saying, "He needs hospital not jail." Gary would override the detective and direct him to arrest the user. Gary never knew the reasons for the detective's mood and attitude swings until now.

Sitting in the gutter, Gary had flashbacks. He recalled there was a time when they were all sitting in the Detective's meal room. They'd done a drug raid and were having a rest. "When we entered into the house on the raid, we whipped off the bedclothes to make sure there was nothing hidden, like guns, knives or drugs. In the meal room we were all laughing that two of the drug dealers were caught naked. 'Caught with their pants down' as they say. During the joking and laughing, this particular detective walked out and slammed the door. No one could work out why he stormed out."

Looking back, Gary realised the detective took what they all thought as funny, the opposite way. Very insulting because his brother was a drug addict. He had taken the jokes personally. He was hurting and grieving and they didn't know.

It was then the detective in the gutter spoke to Gary, He said, "My brother is dead, he overdosed today."

He expressed disappointment in his brother. He told Gary how, at one stage his brother had thought of joining the police force. He then said to Gary, "Come in and meet the family."

Gary went in and had a cup of tea with the family, who were grieving. Gary listened to them for about an hour and was preparing to leave. Gary said to the detective, "Before I leave, I'll have a word of prayer." Gary says they knelt around the coffee table and prayed to God and asked for comfort for the family. Gary had a small biblical tract, which he gave to the detective as he left. Gary contacted the rest of the detectives to give them the news and to support their mate.

Next morning Gary rang the detective to see how he was getting along. Gary asked him, how things were.

He said, "We're getting there. We're coming to grips with it. It has helped me to trust in Jesus to forgive my sin and to forgive the way I thought."

He then broke into laughter. Gary said, "What's funny?"

He replied, "When you left last night my father said, "Thank you very much son for bringing that priest into our house last night. Thank you very much for bringing him in to see us. He brought God's love into our lives."

I said, "Dad, that's not a priest, he's my Detective Sergeant. I work with him, he's my boss."

"He can't be a cop son, he prayed in our home last night just like a priest."

Gary had a good laugh as well. He certainly saw he funny side of it. Gary says people wonder how you can be a cop and a Christian at the same time. It's easy really. People think during the week you charge around with a gun in a police car and then on Sunday you change personality and go to church and become an 'altar boy'. But the fair dinkum Christian is a Christian all week. Gary says he realised this when he became a Christian cop. He saw himself as a Christian minister in a blue uniform. He's never seen a difference between being a cop and a Christian. The task of the police is to rescue people, and this is also the task of the Christian.

A Murdered Baby
A fellow and his wife had a newborn baby. The father was suffering from anxiety and alcoholism. One night in a violent alcohol fuelled rage he began to assault his wife when she refused him sex. In his rage, he pulled the baby out of its cot by the ankles and used the baby to hit the woman. The baby hit the lounge room wall. The man in his rage continued to hit the baby on the floor.

When paramedics arrived, they discovered the baby had no signs of life. The mother was taken to hospital with injuries and shock. The man left the house and took off. Gary and the late Detective Sergeant Bob Broad arrived with Forensic Scientists. Crime scene police officers were crying as details were given. At this stage, the offender had not been arrested.

They had to put a tag on the baby's ankle and then send the body off to the mortuary in a zipped up body bag. Having to do this was doubly hard for Gary because he and his wife Michelle were having difficulty in conceiving a child. Gary as a child was inflicted with a virus which took out his ability to become a father; not a fully functioning man of course, but couldn't conceive a child. They were seeking advice from a medical team, without success. Here in the middle of their struggle to produce a baby, was a fellow who had actually killed his baby. This made it doubly hard for Gary, although all the people at the scene were extremely upset.

It was a clear night outside the crime scene. Gary found himself alone. The stars were shining. Gary was diverted as he looked up into the heavens and said to himself, "God, we can't have a baby and there's one inside this house on the floor dead. It doesn't make sense or seem right. I love and serve You and don't understand why You let these things happen?"

Just then a strong sense of peace flooded Gary's mind and soul. It was as if God the Holy Spirit said to him, "You can know Me fully. I will reveal Myself to you (John 14:21) however Gary, you won't understand my thoughts as they're higher than your thoughts and my ways higher than your ways (Isaiah 55:8). You won't understand right now, but you can trust Me in everything. You can know from My word—your heavenly Father knows best."

Gary began to cry as he reaffirmed his trust in God even though he didn't fully understand what the future held. Gary knew that God would have told the offender, in his conscience, not to kill his baby but the man disobeyed God and did it against God. "You can't blame God for that", Gary said. Gary returned to the crime scene after wiping away his tears and vigorously blowing his nose. He had a drink of water from a garden hose next door and switched back into Detective Sergeant 'mode'.

Gary and Bob followed the government funeral contractor's vehicle transporting the baby's body to the morgue. They had to cover the continuity of the body from the scene to the coroner and 'book' the body into the morgue. On the way, two intoxicated young men recognised Gary's unmarked police car. They stuck their fingers up at Gary and Bob and in hysterical laughter mouthed the word 'pigs'. Bob, who was driving, slammed his foot on the foot brake, rammed on the hand brake, left the police car quickly, ran at the young men and grabbed them both, pushing them into a metal fence. There was a deep bang. He yelled at them, "How dare you stick your fingers up at us you little mongrels. You see that van in front of our car? That's got a dead baby in it and we are going to put it in a fridge at the morgue."

At this stage, Gary had reached Bob and the young men. Gary pulled Bob off them and told him to get back to the car and calm down. Bob yelled again at the boys, "When was the last time you put a baby in a fridge, you smart bastards? You gutless wonders wouldn't even become cops, let alone do what we have to do. I'll give you stick your fingers up at us."

Gary again told Bob to get back to the car, which he did. Gary said to the young men, "Listen you blokes, my mate is upset at you because you disrespected us. As he said, in the back of that van is a baby that was murdered. We have to do some horrible things as detectives in line with our job. What you did was very insulting to us. Now get home and wake up to yourselves."

Gary returned to the car and the youths left. Bob was very quiet and still angry. At the morgue they did the procedure of booking the baby's body in and returned to the police station.

Jumping ahead for a minute, the next morning Gary and Bob were called to the Superintendent's office. They thought it was to give the boss information about the progress of the murder investigation. It wasn't. The two young men and their parents were sitting in the office. Gary and Bob thought they were in trouble for confronting the boys. They sat down. Both boys, in tears, apologised to Gary and Bob for their behaviour the night before. They expressed sorrow for insulting the police, not knowing what police work was really like. Both sets of parents also apologised for their son's antics. The boys asked what they could do to make amends.

TIME FOR TEARS

Gary said, "Thanks guys, we appreciate you coming in. I apologise too for the way we confronted you."

Bob said, "Yes I do too. I was very upset over the murder and shouldn't have shoved you both into the fence."

Both boys disagreed and said they deserved a wakeup call, which they sure got. Gary said, "You know boys, the best thing you blokes could do is to join the cops and help us in these awful things we have to do."

After a cup of coffee they left. Gary and Bob were so relieved they didn't get into trouble over the matter. Gary and Bob were delighted some years later when they saw both the boys in full police uniform. They had actually taken Gary's and Bob's advice and joined the cops. They all had a good laugh over the events of that night in the past, this time as fellow mates together in the police.

Getting back to the murder, the offender was located and arrested later than night. He had sobered up. Bob and Gary interviewed him. He was very upset when the gravity of what he had done dawned on him. He was shaking and crying, explaining he 'did his block' when the baby took precedence over him with his wife's time and attention. He said he got jealous and resented what he perceived as getting 'left out in the cold'. Gary and Bob charged him with murder.

As Gary was typing, the offender, in tears said, "I'll burn in hell for this, won't I?"

Gary replied, "Only if you don't repent to God of your life's entire sin mate, including this."

"What do you mean?"

"When Jesus died on the cross, He had you and what you did in mind and forgave you."

"Even, for what I did?"

"Yes, even that. He forgave us all, for all our sin, every one of them."

The man gently slipped off his chair, knelt on the floor in the interview room and begged Jesus Christ to forgive him. Gary then prayed for him. Later, he was placed in the cells for the night. He was eventually convicted of manslaughter and spent a lengthy time in jail. He became a strong Christian and a new man. There is not a day that goes past that he doesn't regret what he did. He and his wife eventually got back together and have two children. They both attend church regularly.

Gary said, "Many people can't believe that God would forgive a murderer. They think that there are 'bad' sins and 'not so bad' sins. That's not true. The Bible says that sin is sin and has made us fall short of God's glorious ideal (Romans 3:23). All sin, no matter what, offends God and condemns us. We can't justify our sin by saying, "It wasn't that bad or not as bad as other people" (1 John 1:8). We can't say we're good and someone else is bad (Romans 3:10). We are all sinners in need of a Saviour. His name is Jesus. He wants murders, adulterers, thieves, blasphemers, liars to surrender to His love and forgiveness. That's you and me."

Too Young to Die
Gary was Duty Officer at Blacktown. It was the time when he was called to a scene at local park in Doonside where a youth was found hanging in a rope, by the neck, from a tree. When Gary arrived, a police officer had cut him down (preserving both knots) and was attempting resuscitation. A wallet in the back pocket gave a name and address. An ambulance crew arrived and placed a defibrillator on the chest. The monitor showed a flat line. Sadly, death had struck.

Even so, they still tried to get the heart active with drugs. This did not work. The forensic people were called in. The area was taped off as a crime scene. Gary went to the address provided in the wallet taken from the dead youth.

Gary knocked on the door. A fairly big Caucasian gentleman came to the door. Gary said, "I need to speak with you. May I come in please?"

"Something's wrong isn't it? the man replied"

TIME FOR TEARS

"Yes it is."

Gary showed him the wallet and its contents. The man's wife came up the hallway. She had an apron around her waist and a tea towel. As she arrived in the lounge room she said, "It's my youngest son isn't it?"

"Do you have a son?"

"I have three sons, twenty, eighteen and fourteen."

The man said, "My fourteen year old, it's his wallet, he's dead isn't he?"

Gary was sitting on their lounge. They were on lounge chairs with a coffee table in between.

"Oh no, he's dead."

Gary said, "I'm so sorry, he is."

There was silence. Then they cried out. There was a flood of tears. The father said, "I told him never to drive a car. It was a car accident wasn't it? When did it happen?"

"It wasn't a car accident, Sir."

The man looked puzzled.

"Oh God, I told him never to take drugs. It was drugs wasn't it?"

"No, it wasn't drugs."

"He was murdered? Did you get who did the person who did it?

"No Sir, he wasn't murdered."

Then he almost yelled,

"What happened then Inspector?"

"Sir, he suicided and we found him hanging in a tree from a length of rope down the road in the park."

"What?" He yelled.

The wife sobbed uncontrollably.

The man just stared at Gary. Then he started to breath heavily and puffing his cheeks. Gary could see his neck muscles going in and out. Suddenly he got up, skirted around the coffee table, grabbed Gary by his jacket, half shook Gary and pulled him up from his sitting position.

"Inspector, don't tell me my son suicided. Tell me he was killed in a car accident, murdered or took drugs, but don't tell me he suicided. For God sake, no."

Gary was not frightened when the man grabbed his jacket as he knew it was a 'grief' response. The father started crying uncontrollably and let Gary go. Gary then carefully and slowly pulled the father towards him and cuddled him. As he let go and cried, tears poured down his face onto Gary's police jacket.

Gary gestured to the man's wife to come over. She stood up and Gary cuddled them both together. The three cried together. Gary deeply hurt for them both. They stood for about ten minutes just crying. Gary started praying for them speaking quietly next to their ears. Finally, they all composed themselves. They hugged each other again.

Gary went to the kitchen and made them a cup of coffee each and one for himself to allow time for them to speak to each other alone. By this time, they sat together on the lounge. Their hands shook so much, the coffee spilt. Then they started asking each other why he would suicide? He and his girlfriend recently broke up. This was probably it.

The father asked,

"Did he leave a note?"

"No, Sir he didn't."

"Well, we'll never know."

The mother said, "Inspector could you have made a mistake? Was he murdered?"

"There's nothing to indicate foul play. There will be an autopsy. The forensic team say it was suicide but there will be further investigation. Our people want to know, it's not just another case."

They talked about why. Gary discovered the youth had listened to 'goth' music. He'd also broken up with his thirteen-year-old girlfriend and he'd consumed some alcohol.

Gary explained that the body had gone to Westmead Coroner's Mortuary. He said one or both parents needed to go to the mortuary to identify the body. They put on some warm clothes and Gary drove them to the mortuary. Gary could see the stunned mother's face in the car mirror. The husband asked a number of detailed questions. In such a case, Gary was well aware you can't say too much until the autopsy. Both parents were disturbed and shaking.

Then father said, "I told him, you do stupid things when you drink."

The mother calmed him down by saying, "It's too late for that."

After the body identification, Gary took the parents back to their home where relatives and neighbours were waiting to lend support. Both cuddled Gary and thanked him sincerely for seeing them through one of the hardest parts of their life so far. At the time of the suicide, a party was going on across the park. Gary asked for police to meet him there to make enquiries.

When Gary and police arrived, someone asked, "Has something happened?"

Gary said, "I'm sorry to say a young boy suicided in the park earlier."

The young people present screamed. It took a while for Gary to calm them down. The police found seven or eight teenagers in a drunken state.

One girl screamed, "Not true. I'll find him." As she ran out of the house two police officers chased after her and brought her back, punching and screaming. Finally, information came to hand that the young man who suicided had fought with his girlfriend and walked out, threatening suicide. No one followed him. A nearby garage had been broken into and some rope had been stolen. This was identified as the rope used in the hanging.

Gary reflects that this case was one of the saddest he has dealt with. To see the anxiousness on people after a suicide is disturbing. He says people must become suicide prevention aware and look for people in that frame of mind after a depressing event and offer them professional help.

CHAPTER FIVE
VIEWS FROM THE BEAT

"Law enforcement officers are never 'off duty.' They are dedicated public servants who are sworn to protect public safety at any time and place that the peace is threatened. They need all the help that they can get." *Barbara Boxer*

On Criminals
"What do criminals look like? If they looked like those shifty characters in Hollywood movies, straight out of central casting, chances are they wouldn't get away with their crimes." Derrick Hand 'The Coroner' (Derrick worked in the New South Wales Court System for 47 years)

Regarding the common criminal, Gary says, "When it comes to the signs of a common criminal, they are very hyper vigilant. Eyes are going to and fro all the time because most criminals are people on drugs and have lots of enemies. They rob each other, rip each other off, assault each other and so they're always eager to pay each other back in violence. money, drugs or other favours. They move quickly between points by foot or vehicle. Usually the vehicles are stolen or heavily defected.

"They don't have driver's licences. You and I stroll around; they move more quickly because they're on a mission. They are either out to steal something, find drugs, a place to sell their stolen goods. They are constantly looking for associates. They are often sweaty or clammy, skinny, medically sick and malnourished. Their eyes are often glazed or red. Junkies are on the nod (finding it difficult to stay awake). They stand up quickly and get unsteady on their feet. If on uppers they talk fast, on downers they talk slowly. They are excellent liars and extremely manipulative.

"You can tell they've been in jail because they're fit. They go to gym in jail and just pump iron most of the day. Their tattoos are poor artwork and usually in one colour, usually blue. They look poorly impregnated into the skin for they're done with biro pen ink, often in the most inappropriate places like neck, face, fingers, knuckles and toes. Sometimes burnt with a hot needle or pin.

"Mind you, they look different when they come to court to impress. Manipulative behaviour at its best. It's a case of 'I look good' so 'I must be good'. Some females wear makeup to cover fighting scars or plain glass spectacles to look educated. If hair has been dyed, they will re-dye it to normal. They will get rid of jewellery. Women will over dress. In court, their dress will be down to the knees. They will even take a baby into Court hoping the judge will feel sorry for them. They will even put on a crying spree. They will give family a hard time one day and beg them to be in the courtroom the next.

"They will 'con' agencies like the church to say they have been well behaved and that they have reformed. All such things are known as 'tricks of the trade' to face court. Some women will even make out they are breast feeding when they are bottle feeding. Men and women wear a long-sleeved shirt to cover tattoos. They will often turn themselves into the victim and blame the real victim for the offence. They always accuse police of mistreating them. It's part of the discredit the police process. They will provide information to the defence counsel regarding their poor background.

"They will blame their background, their alleged dysfunctional mother or father, their lack of education, the bad people they hang around with and many more excuses or reasons for their behaviour. There are numerous people with bad backgrounds that have never committed an offence. Such things are often not checked by court. Not enough time or resources. They will also say they were sexually assaulted as a child. Such matters are presented in decision making, however they can misuse this as an excuse for committing a crime."

The Justice System and Community Policing
'What do you think of our justice system?

Gary says, "Having listened to the prosecution and defence, nine times out of ten you would agree with the sentence handed down. Given all the facts, most sentences are just and fair. The British Westminster Justice System that we use, really does work. I think we really do have a fair justice system. In the early English days, the community used to take action on criminals themselves. The community would arrest a person in the act of committing or after an offence and take them, and any property found upon them, straight to a justice (magistrate) to be dealt with according to law. The community were the police, as there was no actual police force in those days. In time, the community got lazy and refused to accept responsibility for the apprehension of criminals. They wanted to let someone else do the law enforcement. That's when the community handed over the responsibility to police officers which developed into the modern policing model to find and arrest criminals. The community must cooperate with police to keep the community safe. Not put their head in the sand.

"We talk about malicious damage and have stopped using the term 'vandalism'. We need to prevent graffiti by these vandals. We need to remove the 'tag' straight away for then there's nothing to display, no criminal trophy. Councils need to provide graffiti teams to erase it quickly. Tags are photographed. There's even a tag register—a tag directory.

"In regard to drug growing or manufacturing groups, the outlaw biker gangs take the cake. On television dramas, there are reprisals on informants and witnesses of crime by the score. In the real world, reprisals are rare unless you are in the drug and biker subculture yourself. Reporting crime and giving evidence in court is safe for the community. Giving evidence is a very strong crime prevention and detection tool. There's always the power of the citizen's arrest. You (citizen's arrest) can arrest someone in the act of a crime, or immediately after a crime, immediate pursuit, using reasonable force.

"There is no power to punish the suspect yourself. Even though there is a power to arrest, it's dangerous for many reasons. The suspect may be stronger, have weapons, be crazed on drugs or alcohol, have associates nearby and may have contagious diseases. Follow the suspect, don't chase. Mobile phones are great. Ring 000 and give police your location, the suspect's description and wait for police to arrive. Never corner a criminal or prevent them from getting away. They will fight, even sometimes to the death, to escape.

"The Fire Brigade don't go out looking for fires. No good going straight to the business. Look for the offender first. Let the police know about a person who is taking goods. The police can match people on CCTV by your description. A flicked cigarette butt signals lawlessness. We put hand on machine and can discover if a person is wanted for murder in Queensland. Police deal with Cash Converters. They send in plain clothes detectives and track the sale of stolen goods... Police still plead with the community to identify items. Photographic identity, etch property so it can be linked. If people did this police recovery rate would double.

"Interpol works hard in America and Europe and there is good rapport with Australian police forces. On one occasion, a criminal was taken in for break and entry. It was discovered by bar coding and dot tracing that he did hold ups in Sydney, then flew back to Melbourne every day. He was caught. Bear in mind the police force is catching up with criminals. Every person on earth has a different DNA. The more the community cooperates with police, the safer our communities become."

The Human Touch

While doing a ride-along with Gary, a driver turned suddenly whilst speeding in front of us at a T-intersection. Gary pulled the driver over. It was a female in her thirties. She admitted she was speeding and said she was in a hurry to get her young son to a birthday party. She pleaded, "I was only a little over the speed limit," Then she added, "I'm allowed that aren't I?" "No." was Gary's reply. He said. "Over the limit is over the limit. I'm going to caution you because I don't want to see you or your son in the mortuary today."

Gary wrote particulars in his Police Notebook. The women began to cry. Gary said," What's wrong madam?"

She replied, "When you said the word 'morgue', it hit me in the guts. I got a picture in my mind of my son's dead body, covered in blood, on a stainless steel tray, near a fridge in the morgue. I never thought my actions may lead to that. It's horrible; I can't bear to think about it. I am a fool. I will slow down from now on. Thank you for mentioning the consequences even though it upset me so much."

"Thank you Madam, I hope our encounter today has meant something," Gary said gently.

Gary told me he wishes everyone had such a mind picture of their loved ones in such a place. He said," Police see those things in the morgue frequently. This is the horrible outcome of people disregarding the road rules. You see bent, broken and bloodied bodies in body bags, on the slabs and in the fridges. When autopsies are performed by the Doctor, that's when you really see the extent of the injuries to organs and blood vessels. No wonder they died. Not to mention those burnt to death in collisions. If everyone obeyed the road rules, we would have no collisions."

Gary passionately continued, "I know we can't do it, but I wish I could take every driver on a tour of the morgue and show them the reality of the carnage. It might make them physically sick but think twice about their driving behaviour. In the cops, we call the road, the 'bitumen battlefield'. I would also like to take them on a tour of a Spinal Injury Unit at a major hospital to gaze on those struggling to even wipe their own bum with toilet paper or being fed and bathed. Such a mess is preventable. I suppose some awful individuals will continue to hurt us and them. Never learn.

"The other thing that annoys me is that if a person puts a gun up to someone's head and shoots, they give them life in jail. If someone drives a vehicle drunk, drugged, tired or dangerously ,they get 6 months jail, if that. Where's the justice in that? One killed with a gun and the other a vehicle. It's murder, not an accident. Just ask those left behind to grieve for the rest of their lives."

Also while riding along with Gary in the Blacktown area, we noticed a youth who looked suspicious. He was dressed in camouflage clothes. The youth was ducking and weaving, so to speak, around the streets on foot. He was hiding behind garbage bins, trees, parked cars and running between objects like a 'Commando'. Gary observed him for a while then spoke to him, since there had been a report of a break and enter offence in the area. After questioning him, it turned out the youth was meeting his girl friend to walk her to work. Her parents didn't like him and bitterly disapproved of the relationship, so he was going about hiding to avoid her parents. Gary wondered what sort of future that relationship had.

Gary said, "Proves you need to be a good investigator and be sure before you arrest someone they have actually committed an offence. Sometimes people may act in suspicious ways but they're quite innocent. Those who are mentally ill fall into this category as well. They act strangely sometimes so we get them to professional help."

On more than one occasion Gary was in trouble for being too human or too kind. His supervising Senior Sergeant once said to him, "Gaza, you've got to stop doing your 'social work' stuff whilst on duty. Ministers, the Salvation Army Officers or priests can do that work. Keep your Christian work when off duty."

Gary said, "Okay Serg, no worries, but I'm only trying to help straighten their lives out so they don't get arrested again and go back to jail. It's like crime prevention strategy Serg."

"Okay but you've got to stop doing it at work."

"But Serg, that's where you come across these people in a mess, at work in the police station."

Right at that very second, the Superintendent walked in and said to the Sergeant, "Good morning gentlemen, there's a woman in the cells with lots of needs. Do you mind if I borrow Gary for a while to do some social work? Maybe he can help her or get help for her."

Gary and the Sergeant looked at each other and began laughing hysterically. The Superintendent said, "Anything wrong Sergeant?"

"No Sir, just a private joke with Gary and me. Go on down Gary and see what you can do to help."

"Yes Sergeant, my pleasure," Gary said ,still laughing with his Sergeant.

The Sergeant still can't believe the perfect timing of the Boss's visit.

Gary told me, "God's timing is perfect. The Sergeant was outranked. God will have His way as He is vitally concerned about all of us. I went down to the cells and arranged Salvation Army help for the lady. She was so grateful, when she was released from jail she came to my church and is doing just fine today." Gary went about his social work in the police station as normal but stayed 'undercover' to avoid the Sergeant's 'radar'.

View from the Hearse

Death is a topic, which even Christians seem to shy away from. Since Gary Raymond has dealt with death in many ways, I took the trouble to probe his views. I asked Gary whether, in his ambulance and police careers, he had dealt with death many times.

His reply: "One thing about doing ambulance work and

policing, death is right in your face the whole time. The thing that gets you the most is what little it takes to stop your body, in other words to kill you. Bleeding in an enclosed body space like the head, chest or abdomen can compress organs and kill you. A clot of blood trapped in a vessel in the brain, will stem the flow of blood and kill your brain tissue, giving a stroke or take your life.

"As for the mechanics of death, you can go to an incident on the road where the vehicle is grossly damaged then see the driver or passengers walking around. Other times, a bump on the side of a vehicle, with little damage, and a person dies. So little a force can kill you. Tearing major blood vessels is a problem in crashes, shootings, stabbings or industrial accidents. Chests can be compressed, people drown, overcome by smoke, there is no end to incidents that can take your life. Not to mention murder or suicide.

"Death is no respecter of age. From someone before they are born, to someone in their secondary century; each dies. You can go to a mortuary and see them lying alongside each other. Then there's the Christian aspect. We cannot prolong life. We seem to have the view that we're too good to die. We think it happens to others, but not us. We're almost in denial and disbelief. We put our head in the sand. People don't realise the forces involved in physics. You can have deceleration injury. Jolts put stress and strain on a body, which can dislocate joints, tear organs and cause internal bleeding. Death is the most common thing in life but no one wants to discuss it.

"Now from the Christian view, knowing the book of Genesis helps us understand what death is. The first man and woman, Adam and Eve had a perfect relationship with God. The entire creation was very good. No sin, death, bloodshed or violence. Perfect. Then Adam and Eve disobeyed God and sinned against Him. The God and mankind relationship broke up and the entire creation fell into death and disarray, as it is today. We all have Adam's sinful nature and a rebellious spirit, which puts a big gap between us and God.

"But guess what? God knew and had already arranged to send His only begotten Son, Jesus Christ, to earth as truly and properly God and truly and properly man to fill the gap. He died and rose from the dead to show sin, death and corruption has been defeated. Jesus took the sin and punishment that God had ready for us, onto Himself. It was God's wrath taken out on Jesus, so we can be forgiven and go free. If we repent, trust God and what Jesus did, we receive the gift of eternal life with God."

Gary gave me this example,

"Imagine you're driving along and a Highway Patrol Officer pulls you over.

"What's wrong officer? I'm doing my 80 kph."

"If you look at the sign, it's 60 kph here."

"Oh no! You've got me fair and square, I'm speeding. I disregarded the sign. I did see it."

The officer writes out the Penalty Notice and hands it to you. You take it.

"Officer, I'm so sorry I was speeding. I'll try not to do it again."

"Before you leave driver, give me the ticket back. I'm going to pay the fine for you and take your offences onto my driving record.

"What would you think of that? You would no doubt be grateful and wonder why he paid the penalty for you? That's what Jesus did. You and I offended. He caught us and condemned us but then took our punishment on Himself and took our offences (sin) on His own record. Our record is clean even though we offended. Jesus took it all. I thank Him so much for doing that for me.

"Read the book of John in the Bible. God puts knowledge of Himself within us. We know what's right and wrong. God gives us the ability to obey Him because we love Him and He loves us. God gives us the ability to believe and to know that one day, we're going to be accountable to Him. As to the manner of death, as a police officer I've seen people dead as a result of an action or inaction by another person. There are smelly deaths and non-smelly deaths, fresh death and decomposed death. I've seen it all. However, my faith in God has kept me steady at such times for I know this life is not all there is. There's more and this keeps my joyful within. There's eternal life in heaven then the new earth. How exciting is that?"

I suggested to Gary we include these words from the poem 'The Man in the Glory', He agreed. The Man Christ Jesus.

1 Timothy 2:5

I wake in the morning with thoughts of His love
Who is living for me in the glory above,
Ev'ry minute expecting He'll call me away,
And that keeps me bright all the rest of the day.

George Cutting

Vanishing Samaritans

A news report revealed a 29-year-old Sydney woman known only as 'Aida' in busy Railway Street in Liverpool, Sydney, fought off a man who tried to drag her into a car. Three other men were inside the car waiting for their prey. Dozens of people were around. No one went to Aida's assistance, despite her screams.

Brendan Keilar was shot dead in Melbourne in 2007 when he tried to stop Hells Angels bikie Christopher Hudson from assaulting a woman.

A woman's body was discovered in a house in Sydney where it had lain for eight years. Nobody cared. Even Centerlink and the electricity people did not bother to check up.

Such incidents have the horrible echo of the Anita Cobby killing. Someone is in trouble. People freeze or go their own way.Research has discovered that when someone needs help, and more people gather, the chance of someone helping decreases.

Perhaps people just don't know what to do.

These incidents are referred to as "bystander effect" — or "Genovese syndrome" —Kitty Genovese was stabbed to death in New York in 1964. She screamed for help, but neighbours did nothing. Gary's view of these news reports, and the subsequent vanishing Samaritans offered his comments:

"When offenders are armed, it's not easy to intervene. Some Samaritans obtain a weapon themselves and engage the offender in a deadly fight to rescue the victim. Samaritans may yell and scream at the offender to distract them away from the victim. Others will monitor the situation and wait for police to arrive. People fear reprisal by way of assault or property damage if they interfere during a crime. Payback is rare but movies and TV make it seem it happens all the time. This puts false fear into people. The community must stick together and back each other up. Only then will our safety and security be guaranteed.

"I have seen many acts of courage by members of the community, going into situations that have threatened their life. Emergencies happen very suddenly, without warning, so people have to respond on instinct, often disregarding their own safety. I believe the days of chivalry are still here. Despite the examples above, many victims of crime and other emergencies owe their lives to Good Samaritans. Many people overcome by smoke in fires have been rescued by passers-by or neighbours. Even off duty police, ambulance or fire fighters have stepped up to the mark without their normal equipment available to do the task. You learn to improvise when away from work."

How does a policeman become a Christian? How does a policeman work as a Christian?

Gary says, "You've got to be tough to be involved in such a wide range of events such as those facing a police officer. When I walked through the gates of the police Academy at Redfern, the Drill Sergeant in charge said, "Those of you, who are not prepared to give your life in the cause of policing, walk out of the front gate now". It is one of the greatest acts of courage for a person to walk through the Academy gates and offer their life to the community as a police officer, not knowing what the future holds.

"When it comes to policing, it's not just what you see, it's what you smell, hear, touch or even taste. You have to prepare for all of that. I was fortunate in being an ambulance officer for 5 years as I was exposed to heavy trauma prior to joining the police. It stood me in good stead preparing me for the things I would experience as a cop. These are the things that impact on you emotionally. There are the nasty things that are said to you by angry people, especially in this day an age where there has become an almost disregard for authority in some undisciplined members of society. Cops are just ordinary people who are called to do extraordinary things."

"At that time I joined the Police Rescue Squad, there were about 10,000 police officers in New South Wales. Only six were in the Police Rescue Squad. I was chosen to be the seventh. I was so thrilled. I had left the Ambulance Service to go to Police Rescue. A dream comes true. We were called upon to do things others couldn't or wouldn't do. I realised when I joined there was no 'Rescue Squad to rescue the Rescue Squad'. We were an elite unit which had many people relying on our skills of rescue and recovery."

Of the hundreds of Rescues you carried out while you were in the Rescue Squad. Which was the riskiest?

Gary responded, "Sadly, a man jumped to his death off The Gap in Sydney. The Gap is near the south peninsula (head) of Sydney Harbour. It is a notorious place for people to end their lives. It was a cloudy, windy day with massive, high seas. We saw the body on the rock platform below, not far from the water line. The waves crashed over the rocks and over the body. The first thing I did was to descend and take a ladder stretcher with me. This timber framed stretcher can be used on the end of a rope or slide up and down a ladder.

"I knew I could not afford to wait, otherwise the waves would wash the body off the rock platform into the turbulent white water. The Water Police vessel could not get in close due to high seas. The body would be lost under the hollow rock platform.

"The waves coming in underneath created what was known

as the big washing machine. In the past, anglers had been swept in there and drowned. We knew from experience how dangerous and violent it was in that white water. Bodies washed in there had come out days later, stripped naked of clothes, even shoes and socks due to the power of the swirling water. There was the risk I could be swept off the platform and plunged into the washing machine unless I was extremely careful. We quickly erected the Cliff Rescue Machine. It was a derrick with a luffing jib used to lower and raise people over cliffs or other heights. Manpower lowered and raised the rope.

"I descended and landed about 15 metres from the body. I detached my safety harness from the stretcher, walked over and knelt beside the body. I checked for vital signs, but they were absent. After brushing off small rock crabs from the body and sending them running, I rolled the body into a heavy plastic body bag and zipped it up. I searched the area for relevant evidence, like a wallet or other ID.

"At that moment, a huge wave crashed in. The water knocked me over and pushed me towards the cliff face, then dragged me back towards the sea. When the water ran out, I was soaking wet and the body had been moved by the waves to the edge of the platform. I started to shiver being both wet and cold. I grabbed the body bag, dragging and rolling it onto the stretcher. I lashed the body onto the stretcher with the stretcher ropes.

"I was just about to attach my safety harness onto the stretcher when suddenly, I felt a surge of water underneath me. I was engulfed in a gigantic wave. The stretcher, body and I were lifted by the wave into the air. The stretcher was under the water as was half my body. I desperately clung onto the stretcher with both hands. I knew that if I let go, I'd come cracking down onto the rocks and end up in the washing machine off the edge of the platform. As the water swept back out across the platform, the stretcher started to quickly drop down.

"I could see myself crashing onto the rock platform and breaking bones. Knowing I'd be seriously injured if that happened, I threw myself face down on top of the body and 'rode' the stretcher down as we crashed onto the rock platform. I felt a hard jolt, which nearly winded me. I heard a loud crack and at the same time, I was sucked towards the edge of the platform on top of the stretcher. It came to rest. I managed to attach my safety line to the stretcher.

"I was now clear of the water and could see the side of the stretcher had been completely snapped off by the fall onto the rocks. I grabbed the side of the stretcher and made sure the body was still strapped on tightly. My squad mates then hurriedly raised me on the rope with the stretcher just as another big wave crashed on the rocks underneath me. That was another close call. I was finally hauled to the top where I was safe at last. Wet and shaky I rested before helping to pack up the equipment.

"I was proud when the late Sergeant Bill Fahey said to me, "Good job Gaz. A real hard one. At least we can get the bloke's body back to his family thanks to your brave work. Good lad. Good we got the busted bit of the stretcher back. Don't know if we'll fix it? I doubt it."

Gary told me, "I knew that if it wasn't for the Lord, I would have ended up with broken bones, drowned or have been dragged into the washing machine, maybe lost forever like some. It may sound awful to others but the body of the man who jumped that day acted as a buffer, like cushion between the rocks and me, saving my life. Strange how the dead can sometimes save the living."

The Police Force
You served the New South Wales Police Force for 34 years. What have you to say about the force?

Gary responded, "It was a magnificent career. I found it satisfying and challenging every inch of the way. As a Christian, it was a continuous blessing to minister to other cops, victims, witnesses and criminals. My wife Michelle was an incredible support to my police career. She was a great listener and backed me up when I had to do things which were traumatic. Because I was a specialist both in the Rescue Squad and later Detectives, I was constantly on call, which ate into our personal time. It wasn't easy but we did it together.

"When it comes to policing in Australia, each state is responsible for law and order within their state. The presence of the police force provides what is virtually a para-military force to prevent crime, keep the peace, apprehend offenders and ensure there's law and order in our society. In normal circumstances, this protection is satisfactory for the purpose of protecting life and property, provided the human resource strength of the police force is adequate and the numbers are not allowed to drop to a dangerously low figure. We also need adequate funding to cover our business model.

"Firstly, the general community doesn't see the wide ambit of the police force. They just see the police driving around and booking motorists. The police do a great deal more, like rescue work and public education. These days, a police officer needs to be a negotiator, social worker, conflict resolver, rescuer, teacher, parent, nurse and much more.

"At a public meeting with the community and government officials at Cabramatta years ago, they said to me, "What can we do about the junkies and street kids at night?"

I replied, "After hours, police are left with all the problems of the world. Everyone else is in a nice warm bed. Other agencies should have shift workers like we do. Police are the only ones available. Those who misbehave are out after dark. It should be a multi-agency approach. Police often have to do tasks well beyond their charter at night because everyone else has gone home. There is constantly the need to get such people into the hands of those who can help for instance, medical and mental health services.   We need social workers on night shift working alongside the police.

"In neighbourhood meetings there were often complaints about kids throwing stones, doing graffiti, wrecking mailboxes and much more. I used to ask, "Do you keep a lookout in your street and report suspicious activity to the police?" Some would say, "No". "Well, how can the police help if you people don't tell the police about it? The police want to interact with people, but it must be a 'two way' street."

Gary continued, "Many people think the police are like ambulance and fire officers who are just sitting around their station waiting for things to happen. Not so with police. We are pro-active and deliberately patrol looking for offenders. The fire brigade people don't go out looking for fires, the ambulance people don't go out looking for sick people and accidents, but police do look for trouble. Police patrolling in police cars do not contact people face to face unless they stop and interact. We need to break down the barriers and interact with the community more in conversation. Foot patrol and bicycle police do help.

"When I was Commander at Manly Police Station I conducted an experiment. I sent two uniformed police constables walking up and down the Manly Corso CBD for an hour. No talking to anyone, just walking. We surveyed business owners, managers and employees with a question, "Have you seen any police activity today?" Most answers were "No", as no one noticed the police as they passed by. Next day, I sent the same two uniformed police along the Corso again. This time, they were to enter all the businesses and speak face to face with the people there. On a new survey, this produced a 99% positive response.

"People knew there was police activity. Not only that, valuable information was exchanged between the people and the police. The community was safer. We also sent Crime Prevention Officers to advise people on crime prevention and safety issues. I discovered that when this happened, people connect with the police, giving a high level of cooperation and networking."

Gary says he believes in the American policing model of having volunteer police officers that watch specific areas. They are uniformed, trained and equipped as police but perform duty outside their normal occupations, like volunteer ambulance officers or fire fighters. Some might disagree with volunteer police, but it would place lots more eyes and ears on the street in a cost effective way. People would feel safer. Perceptions of safety and security count in the community. Another idea was to have people watching the streets for an hour at a time. Like trained observers doing shifts.

Gary said, "When I was at Riverstone Police Station, there was trouble in the central business district at night. Shopkeepers were getting sick of vandalism and theft. People felt unsafe with drunks causing trouble." Gary came up with an ingenious scheme. He met with the shopkeepers and explained: "I want you in pairs to hide in your shop in the dark and be 'look-outs' in the CBD. When you see suspicious activity, ring the police station and we'll send a car to investigate. Stay hidden; don't let the suspects see you."

The first night of 'Operation Nightwatch' was a resounding success. There were 16 shopkeepers and friends hiding in their shops. That amounts to 32 eyes and 32 ears monitoring the area. Some youths kicked over garbage bins. The people watching called police who soon nipped it in the bud. The youths were stunned when the police described their behaviour accurately. "Where were you?" they asked. Other drunks and anti-social behaviour incidents were reported by the watchers and police attended. On one occasion, the owner of the lawn mower shop saw a man steal his large canvas advertising banner. He was arrested by police only 2 minutes later. After just 3 weeks of Friday and Saturday night watching, bad behaviour drastically reduced. The word on the streets was offenders thought police had 'hidden' cameras all over the place or even a satellite watching them from space. They had no idea the 'undercover' shopkeepers and police had a very effective way of 'spying' on them.

Another outcome was that the shopkeepers were able to see police in action first hand. This gave them an appreciation of what police do and how they do it. They passed this information on to the rest of the community, which was great public relations for Gary and his team.

Gary relates his experiences at Wetherill Park. He realised there needed to be interaction between the police and the public. At first, there was a refusal by people to attend police meetings to discuss policing in the community. This attitude was broken down by Gary, who went about door-knocking and meeting people in their homes. He had so many coffees and teas, not to mention the great Asian and European cakes. It's all part of doing his job of course. As a result, Gary was able to try innovative approaches. Things were in good shape. Meetings became well attended and crime prevention education was done.

When Gary was a Duty Officer at Cabramatta, he had a good bunch of young Constables on board. They were very pro-active and were right in the face of street drug dealers. In addition, police with forensic skills were being deployed locally. This increased the arrest rate dramatically as offenders were caught quickly on fingerprint or DNA evidence obtained from the scenes of crime. Gary realised some of the past methods did not work. They made people less likely to tell police of criminals because of their Asian culture of fear. They needed reassuring that unlike Asia, police here can be trusted and would not take bribes or bash them. Gary needed to comfort them that police were opposed to gangs not working with them, again like Asia. In time, the trust grew and things improved.

Looking back, Gary said when he was at Redfern Police Station, the Senior Sergeant said, "Get out there and bash a few heads together". Gary didn't mind a fight but felt uncomfortable just bashing people for nothing. As an ambulance officer, Gary had picked up many people who had been assaulted. Their injuries were sometimes horrific. The 'king hit' is not a modern phenomena; Gary saw it years ago. Bashing heads didn't work for it created animosity against the police. There was deep resentment for police, especially amongst Aboriginals. That has improved now with the police and the Indigenous community getting together and cooperating.

When it comes to law enforcement, people ask exactly what it means. It means exactly that: law enforcement, and no more and no less. However, the administration of law enforcement is dependent on several factors; the passing of legislation by State Parliament to ensure that police have the power to carry out their duties. The police must be supported by the court system, an effective police recruiting scheme and recruits who are well trained. For the police force to function satisfactorily there must be a strong strain of character among the police leadership at all levels.

Once any of these factors is allowed to slip, then the strength of the overall police force starts to suffer. Looking at the current police force in New South Wales, one can consider the administration. Over the years, the administration has become complicated. The question of 'red tape' and excessive 'paper work' has infiltrated the force so that what was once a straightforward system has become complex and time-consuming. Hours are wasted by police creating records that will never again be accessed. The creation of specialist branches has depleted the run of the mill everyday policing. There are now specialist elite units. Such units may be all very well but while they serve special demands, they have nevertheless depleted the front line police.

There is nothing more desirable than a strong frontline force to keep law and order in society. In regard to local policing, this is an area which has grown almost beyond belief in recent years. Police numbers have not however been increased enough and without 24-hour police stations, the police presence has been greatly diminished to the detriment of public safety. In many areas of our state, police presence is negligible. At the time of writing, take for instance the area of Wollondilly. At night, one car covers from Camden to Bargo. The responsibility for this lies fairly and square in the lap of the political arm of the State. Money of course is the source of the problem. The more politicians shrink and plunder the moneybag meant for police, so they weaken the strength of the force.

Having rubbed shoulders many times with the legal profession, Gary relates his experiences: "In regard to the legal profession, most police officers these days, certainly in New South Wales, have good regard for solicitors, although, some are efficient and some are hopeless. The police get frustrated when they apprehend an offender and the offender is released immediately on bail. Many of the bail applications for refused bail are strong, however they get bail with conditions which can and are often broken. In my opinion, the victim suffers greatly when the offender gets bail and it seems few people care. The fear of payback is ever present.

"Some have to be protected by police or move to another State. The victim has no say until final sentencing is taking place. That could be 3 years down the track given the hopelessly slow system we have. Recently in the widely publicised case of Nigella Lawson, she complained she had no say in court."

After half a lifetime in the New South Wales Police Force, one former police officer looked back and said, "I suppose there's no best or worst in half a lifetime spent in the force. It's a difficult and unnatural job at the best of times. When things go well there's the feeling of satisfaction and when they don't, professionalism helps to fight another day. Certainly, every police officer has their Achilles heel. Mine was children!"

In regard to police recruitment, some unsuited people are being recruited. For a start, recruits must have university credits before they can enter the Police Academy at Goulburn. Is that the best way to go? Practical street training before university would weed out unsuitable people before they spend time and money going to university. With the present system, recruits get to a police station and are found lacking in their practical skills. In other words, more hands on training before university. No more square pegs in round holes.

CHAPTER SIX
STRANGE WAYS

"The only normal people are the ones you don't know very well." *Joe Ancis (Comedian)*

Muddled Sexes

Patrolling late one night near the taxi rank at Blacktown Railway Station, Gary saw a big man bashing a woman. He was the aggressor and was getting the upper hand. Gary called for assistance on his police radio and then pulled the aggressor away from his victim. After a struggle, Gary finally grabbed the bloke, but he resisted arrest and wanted to continue punching the woman. They were both Pacific Islanders.

Realising the size of the man, Gary quickly used his foot to kick the legs of the man out from under him, causing him to fall heavily to the footpath. Gary turned him on his stomach then straddled his body and sat on his buttocks. The struggle continued. The man's wrists were so big Gary could only just squeeze the handcuffs on to the first ratchet.

Gary stood up, knelt beside him and held his shoulders down with both hands. Gary bent his arms forward and twisted the handcuffs trying to stop the man resisting. To make things worse, the victim started to kick the offender whilst he was on the ground. Gary pushed her away several times before she sat on the footpath crying and swearing. Other police arrived.

Gary called an ambulance which took the female victim

to hospital. The man was placed in a caged police vehicle and transported. Another police officer followed the ambulance to get a statement from the woman at the hospital. Gary obtained some witness statements from taxi drivers. Gary, exhausted, went back to Blacktown Police Station. The Custody Sergeant greeted Gary.

He said, "Mr Raymond that was a good arrest, that bloke you got for the domestic assault."

Gary said, "Yes, I drove right on to it—saw the lot."

The Sergeant laughed hysterically and said, "Mr Raymond, do you have an eyesight problem?"

"No, why?"

"Do you know the difference between a man and a woman Mr Raymond?"

"Yes, why do you ask?" Gary paused, gave a funny look as the Sergeant said hysterically,

"You know that bloke you arrested? He's got breasts and other female parts. Guess what, Mr Raymond? He is actually a she!"

"Mate, you're having me on. Fair dinkum?" Gary joined the laughter. A number of cops also joined in. It was pandemonium at Gary's expense.

"We looked up the details on the police computer and verified who she is," he explained. "When I talked to her she told me her gay partner and she had an argument over another sheila. She's the 'husband' in the relationship."

Gary said convincingly, "She sounded like a He, looked like a He, acted like a He and sure fought like a He!"

The word rapidly got around the Police Station that Mr. Raymond had a gender identity crisis. Diagrams appeared on the meal room notice board of a man and women saying, "Information for Mr Raymond. Arrows indicate person's gender. This is a man and this is a woman."

Staff would stop Gary in the corridors of the station and comment, "Hello, Mr. Raymond. I just want to make sure you know what gender I am in case you get mixed up. I'm a girl, (then pointing to another officer) he's a boy."

Another police officer using finger gestures said, "Mr Raymond, girls have these, boys have these."

Another Sergeant said, "A married man of your age and experience should know the difference between a man and a woman by now Mr Raymond."

Every time Gary brought in an offender into the station and the gender was entered in the custody records, the Custody Sergeant would say, "Now Mr. Raymond, are you sure of the sex of this person, given your track record?"

From that day on Gary was very diligent to get it right. Humour is a huge part of police work. It gives light relief to a dark world. Gary always took the 'mickey' out of his mates for the mistakes they made on the job. There was always something to amuse the cops every shift. It also makes a great night at station and class reunions when everybody reflects, "What about the time..........." Gary told me that after such get-togethers, he comes home with a sore jaw from laughing all night.

Strip Search on Road
Around midnight there was a call to the police at Blacktown. It was an armed hold up alarm at a petrol station at Doonside. A hold up alarm is where a worker behind the counter presses a button to say they've been threatened by a robber. It's a silent alarm which goes through to a security company who contact police. Gary and another police officer responded to the call and when they were approaching the intersection of Kildare Road and Lancelot Street, they were startled to see and narrowly miss a man lying in the middle of the intersection. The police car narrowly missed the man, who was motionless. A pushbike lies beside him on the road.

Gary's immediate thought was, "This poor man has been knocked down and left to die in the middle of the road. The offending driver has driven away. Gary radioed for an ambulance and instructed the other police cars to continue to the hold-up alarm.

Gary and his mate got out of the police car and walked over to the man. Gary with his ambulance officer training began to examine the extent of the man's injuries. He was unconscious but Gary couldn't find any obvious injuries. The two police officers carefully rolled the man into a recovery position, making sure his neck and spinal column stayed straight. Gary maintained the man's airway until the arrival of the ambulance officers.

As they were examining the man, they tested his level of consciousness by testing his pain response. Much to Gary's surprise the man quickly woke up and Gary saw him turn his head and clutch his fist ready to punch the ambulance officer who was kneeling beside the man. Gary jumped in and forcefully pulled the ambulance officer away. Gary grabbed the man's arm, twisted it behind his back and with the other police officer, handcuffed the man. The man was yelling, cursing and swearing. By this time the man was fully alert and at the same time most abusive.

Gary put on his police gloves and started to search for weapons. As he did so, he came across a large number plastic bags containing marijuana in his pockets. The ambulance officers finished their examination and gave the man the all clear. They realised the man didn't get hit by a vehicle after all. He had fallen asleep whilst riding his pushbike after smoking lots of marijuana. He had fallen off his bike and slept in the middle of the road! How fortunate Gary found him and not a semi-trailer! Gary had experienced many events during his time as a police officer, but this event just about beat the lot.

Gary searched the man's backpack and found it too was full of marijuana in bags and a freshly used bong. Gary called for a caged police vehicle and the man was taken to Blacktown Police Station. The armed hold up alarm turned out to be false. The cashier at the petrol station had accidentally set off the alarm.

On his return to the police station, Gary informed the offender that because of drugs found on him, he would be thoroughly strip searched for further drugs that might be hidden around or in his body. As the man sat in the prisoners dock area, he was bleary eyed, sleepy, quite abusive and full of insults toward the police.

Gary then told the man to take his shoes and socks off and take his overalls off prior to the search. With this command, the man became extremely sarcastic and accused the police of getting some pleasure from him undressing. Gary then asked the man to squat and spread the cheeks of his buttocks so there could be a full inspection to ensure there were no hidden drugs.

The man began to speak loudly and said, "Oh, you want to see my bum? Do you and your police mates get a thrill looking at people's backsides? I know your type."

Gary replied, "Look mate, just do what we directed."

Then the man spread his backside cheeks very wide. He started bouncing up and down yelling, "What can you see? Have a good look. Why don't you get a torch and go for a walk up there? Don't get lost up my clacker!" The man laughed loudly and raucously.

Gary patience started to run out. From a bit of an amusing situation it was turning into a farce. He sternly said to the man, "This is unacceptable behaviour. Put your clothes back on and stop carrying on like this."

With that, the man started to shuffle backwards toward the police officers. He kept on saying, "You want a look. Have a good look. Whatever turns you all on."

Gary then said very assertively, "Listen mate. I'm not sure if you realise your disgusting behaviour is being recorded on the CCTV cameras up there on the ceiling." With that Gary pointed to the CCTV cameras in the charge room and said to the man,

"Mate, if you want to carry on like this you need to know every bit of this is being recorded."

With that the man suddenly froze, held his breath, opened his eyes wide and looked up at the cameras. His mouth dropped. He screamed, "Oh no, you're kidding me aren't you?"

Immediately he stood up, grabbed his underpants, quickly put them on, grabbed his overalls and put them back on. Next he sat on the dock seat and looked around to see where the cameras were and how many there were. He then looked at Gary and said whimpering, "Please Sir, I'm very sorry. I didn't mean it. I wasn't having a go at you, truly. I didn't mean what I said."

He then put his hands together as if in prayer and he pleaded, "Please don't show that on TV. Are you going to give it to the TV channels? If you do, can you block out my face and my buttocks? I'm sorry. What I did was disgusting. Please don't show anyone what I did. I'll never live it down if it goes on TV."

Gary saw his opportunity. He knew the footage would only be used by the police or courts and certainly would not be given to a commercial TV station. But he was not going to tell the offender that after what had happened. Seizing the moment, Gary said to the man, "Look mate. I'm a fair bloke. I'll do a deal: if you sit here and behave yourself and do everything we ask you to do, then I won't show your disgusting behaviour on the TV for everyone to see. Have we got a deal?"

The man said, "Yes Sir you got a deal, thank you so much. I'll do everything I'm told. You're a great bloke and I'll never forget how you've helped me tonight."

Gary said, "That's for sure mate. You're better to end up in police custody than in the city morgue."

Gary had at first thought the man was a drug courier but it became clear that all the marijuana in his possession was for his own personal use. He was charged with possession of the drugs. In his entire police career Gary never had seen anyone with so many drugs for their own personal use. Every bag and pocket was full of them. Talk about stocking up the 'pantry'. Gary gave the man a cup of coffee and had a long talk about the man going into rehab to deal with his drug addiction. The man told Gary he had no intention whatsoever of going into rehab and would continue using drugs for the rest of his life.

Gary could not resist, saying sarcastically, "The next time you're arrested mate you better behave yourself or I'll get your TV show out of storage."

A Bike that Slides

Gary was Duty Officer on this particular day when the Eastern Creek motor races were on. He was responsible for organising the police dealing with matters both inside and outside the race track. Gary decided to head back to the office and do some paperwork while the car races were on. On the way back from the speedway to the Blacktown Police Station, Gary realised it was a beautiful day. He decided to stop beside the road and use his police car computer to catch up on a bit of paperwork. He tapped away on the keyboard.

Just then, out of the corner of his eye, Gary saw something flash past the front of his police car. He looked up and saw a motorcycle catapulting past. It was quickly followed by a young man sliding past on his backside. Both came to rest in the scrub just beyond the left side of the car. Gary had to do a double take to be sure of what he just saw. The rider just sat there. Gary locked up the computer and walked over to the motor bike rider and said,

"Are you okay mate?"

He said, "Yes Sir, I think so." He stood up and staggered around.

Gary noted the rider didn't have leathers on, only shorts. He had quite a few very red raw skin abrasions all over his body as a result. Gary called an ambulance and another police car. The Highway Patrol came. The ambulance crew cleaned, treated and bandaged his abrasions and he was allowed to go home looking like an Egyptian Mummy! Gary was sure the youth would have been very sore for quite a while.

This was not this young man's day. He rode around a bend in the road at high speed. The youth suddenly saw Gary's police car and thought it was a Highway Patrol car conducting radar speed checks. In a panic, he immediately applied his brakes so he wouldn't be booked.

He applied the brakes too hard. The bike came to a sudden stop and slipped out in front of him. He lost control, came off the bike and both slid in front of Gary's police car.

The young man said to Gary, "I thought you were doing radar."

Gary replied, "Sorry mate, this is not your day. I'm not Highway Patrol and I've never had a radar in my hand let alone use it. In addition to that mate, I don't know how to write out a traffic ticket either. I've been in rescue and detectives, not traffic. Finally, I was parked to do some computer work, not catch speeding riders."

The young man said, "You're dead set right, it wasn't my day. Still I've learnt a lesson about speeding." His mate turned up to take him and his damaged bike home.

This was one time when Gary was right on the spot, as it were. He says it just shows how things can happen. Gary said jokingly, "It was one of the best responses I've ever had to an accident. I was there in five seconds."

It was a case of not 'Johnny on the spot' but 'Gary on the spot.' It also proves police visibility does have an effect on motorists! The motor cyclist was given a ticket for negligent riding by the Highway Patrol officer.

Skippy's Wooden Leg
There was a fellow with the nickname 'Skippy.' Skippy had piercing blue eyes, jet-black wavy hair, a black moustache and a goatee beard. He looked a bit like 'Black Beard the Pirate.' He hung around with bikers and petty criminals. He traumatically lost his leg due to a serious motorbike crash. He actually saw his own torn off leg down the road from the scene. There was blood everywhere and God saved him. He was blessed to have lived through that and as a result, he had a prosthesis fitted as a leg. This caused him to run with a wide gait. This meant when he ran he 'skipped' along, hence the nickname.

Skippy became involved in more crime. On one occasion he even escaped from gaol. He'd been arrested a number of times. Gary did his best to get Skippy on the straight and narrow, without success. In trying to get away from the police, Skippy ran. Unfortunately for Skippy sometimes when he ran, his 'wooden' leg fell off. People in the street would be surprised to see a police officer tackle a man and end up holding a leg. Each time Gary arrested Skippy, he spoke to him about where his life was heading. Sadly, Gary felt he wasn't getting through. It seemed Skippy's brain and soul was as 'wooden' as his leg.

Years later, Gary received a phone call at work. Surprise, surprise it was Skippy on the line. He said, "Mr Raymond guess what? I've surrendered to Christ, I'm a committed Christian up in Brisbane and I'm training to do Christian work at the Worship Centre."

Gary was thrilled to bits to see Skippy not now as a criminal but as a brother in Christ.

Skippy said he'd been down and out after being released from jail and went to a church in Brisbane for help. The pastor there led him to Christ. He said many of Gary's past conversations had come back to him, challenged him and resulted in him having a relationship with Christ. Well might we say, 'All's well that ends well'. Gary and Skippy keep in touch even to this day and are great mates. Once they were on opposite sides of the fence but now, both are on the good side of that fence.

The Witches Coven
A call came through with information about an apartment block in Bondi. The apartment was just up from the famous Bondi Beach whose reputation is spread far and wide across Australia and indeed the world. People travel from great distances just to walk on that beach at Bondi. The sand and surf attract like magnets. The police had been told there was a Witch's Coven operating in a unit in the block. An informant told police in a signed statement that had sacrificed babies during satanic ritualistic ceremonies. A Search Warrant was obtained and executed.

Gary and his Police Rescue mates were asked to assist detectives in the search under the unit's floor boards. They ripped up the carpet and floorboards. They dug the soil under unit. The place seemed satanic for it was dark, dingy, had occult symbols and black curtains draped over a sort of altar. There was old blood stains on the altar.

They started to dig for human remains. They dug using a grid pattern and started to find bones. The bones were sifted out from the dirt and set aside for a forensic anatomist to examine. A man, the occupant of the unit, was present. He was dressed in satanic priest's clothes wearing a hug gold chain and satanic symbol around his neck. Gary prayed for time alone with the 'witch' in charge of the coven, He prayed silently, "Lord I want some time alone with this man." Gary was a non-smoker. The other police went out for a smoke and this gave Gary the chance he had prayed for. He was alone with the man.

Gary asked, "What got you into this?"

He said, "I met a friend who introduced me to Satanism. I worked my way up until I found myself in charge of a coven."

"Are you willing for me to talk about Jesus?"

"Yes, I don't mind."

"Where will you go when you die?"

"I guess I'll go to hell, I'll have all my mates there."

"I'd like you to look up what the Bible says about hell, it's a shocking place with no escape. If you do look it up, I guarantee you won't be so frivolous about it."

"God's a big spoil sport. I like doing things that feel good, like sex and drugs. That's Satan's way. "

"They might feel good but they are destructive. That's why God prohibits them. God wants you protected. Not destroy you like Satan will."

"Jesus has done nothing for me."

"Does Satan love you? Did Satan die on a cross to save you? Did Satan rise from the dead to show you he was God? Has Satan promised you salvation, grace, mercy and forgiveness for your sin? Has Satan promised you eternal life without sin, suffering or torment?

"No."

"Then why do you worship him?"

"I'm not sure why."

"You need to read the Bible to compare what you've got and what you can have."

"Yes, you've convinced me, I'll see what the Bible says."

"God has a rescue plan for you. At the moment, you have a ticket to the wrong place. The fact you are willing to talk about it means God is pulling at your heart to surrender to Him."

The man just stood and stared. Then he said, "I've been doing this for a lot of years and it's very empty. I'm not happy."

Gary prayed with the man. He was in tears. Gary gave him his phone number and said, "Don't ignore God's call, it's too dangerous eternally for you. He loves you."

The police returned from their 'smoko' and started digging again. No human bones were found. Chicken bones were found which had been used in sacrifices. Someone had been kicked out of the coven and dobbed the coven in to the police. About 3 weeks later, Gary received a phone call from the 'Satanic witch' saying that he had left the coven and was attending a Christian church in the city. He had read his mother's Bible which he found in a cardboard box in a cupboard left to him after she died. In tears he told Gary he was now free and was safe in the 'arms of Jesus'. He kept in touch. He is now married to a lady from the church and they have two children. He is serving God in ministry in the city.

Gary said," No one is beyond God's reach. No matter whom you are and what you're into, God is calling you to come to Him, through Christ."

Man in Cell with Shaved Head

There was an unearthly racket in a cell at Blacktown Police Station. At the time, Gary was upstairs. At the time, he was also a Detective Sergeant. The phone rang and a voice said, "Gaz, we've got a difficult man down here in custody. He has been arrested for domestic violence. We will do a cell extraction but we want to try negotiation first. Can you help?"

Typically, Gary agreed to do what he could. When he went down to the cell, he saw the man running round and round in the cell naked covered in blood from abrasions on his head after scraping it along the concrete wall. He screamed and yelled the whole time. Gary discovered the man was in for an assault on his wife. They had broken up. He had shaved his head prior to being arrested as a protest over his marriage breakdown. Gary went to the bars of the cell and said,

"Mate, I know why you're doing this, you're scared. You feel helpless and hopeless. You're not angry at us, you're angry about your past. You feel your life is going nowhere."

He yelled, "No one cares for me." Gary said, "God does."

The man started to swear and said, "God's never done anything for me. As a matter of fact, I worship Satan. He's my god."

"What's he ever done for you, except harm you?"

"He gives me drugs."

"Is that all? God can give you love and forgiveness through Jesus who died on the cross for you and rose from the dead to show He is God the Son."

"How do you know?"

"The Bible says it and it can be trusted with the truth. God has given me discernmen; there is demonic activity in you. Evil spirits you will leave this man immediately in Jesus Name."

Gary was confident about his authority as a police officer and even more as a Christian over evil spirits because of God's Holy Spirit indwelling in every true Christian. The man shook, looked down and saw his clothes were off.

He said, "Who took them off?"

"You did."

"I don't remember."

The man began to cry uncontrollably and ask Jesus to forgive him. Gary and the others comforted and reassured him. Gary observed, "Where Jesus doesn't dwell, Satan will." How true.

Gary said, "Come on, I'll get you to have a shower and clean up." Gary then prayed with the man. The other police officers stood there in amazement. Gary had a nickname of 'The People Whisperer' as well as the 'Pink Panther'. Gary always explained to his workmates it was God who worked in people's lives and hearts, not Gary.

Gary and other police escorted the man to the shower and they cleaned him up. An ambulance was called to check him over. He was taken to hospital for head injury observation. He ended up okay. Later, the man was taken to court and convicted of assault. An Apprehended Domestic Violence Order was served on him. Later, after counselling with a chaplain, their marriage was restored and both regularly attend church. They both came to the station to thank Gary and his mates for the understanding and kind treatment during one of their darkest times.

Woman Prostitute on Highway
Gary was patrolling about 3am one morning. He'd spoken to the Christian Street Team who provided prostitutes with something to eat and drink. They told Gary there was a young woman up the road who had refused contact with them and they had great concern for her welfare. Gary drove up the street and spoke to the woman who was dishevelled, droopy eyed, smoking and skinny. Her eyes had sunk into her face. Obviously, she was a drug addict. Gary challenged her with being a prostitute out on the street at this hour. She said,

"I don't care. I want the money and my drugs."

Gary said,"Aren't you worried about the dangers of being out at this hour of the morning?"

"Yes but I don't care."

"Well I do. I don't want to be the one to attend your murder," Gary said quite forcefully but gently: "Listen young lady, I was a detective involved in the investigation of the rape, torture and murder of nurse Anita Cobby just down the road from here some years ago. You need to wake up to yourself ,otherwise God forbid, you could end up like her dead in a paddock somewhere."

With an upset look on her face, she stared at Gary for quite some time. Gary broke the silence and said, "What are you thinking?"

She said, I'm related to John Travers."

Gary was shocked, felt embarrassed and remorseful because he'd mentioned the Cobby murder. Her relative John Travers was the ring-leader of the gang of five. Travers cut Anita's throat whilst she was conscious and killed her. Seeing the young woman was traumatised by his comment. Gary said quietly, "Look, I'm sorry. I didn't know who you were and I didn't mean to upset you. I just wanted to get the message through to you of just how dangerous it is out here. Please accept my apology in one way, but I'm certainly not going to apologise for the warning in another way. I've given it to you to help and save you. So please go down to the Christian Street Team van and allow the ladies down there to give you a lift home. Will you do that?"

She agreed and went down to the van and she was taken home. As Gary continued his patrol he started to flash back to the Anita Cobby murder (which was mentioned in the first *Top Cop* book). Gary had never considered before how the family and friends of the five offenders had suffered as a result of being closely related to those offenders. Who knows how much ridicule they went through because they were related to the murderers and rapists? Who knows the young woman Gary spoke to that night might have been affected by some of those things? When he was a police officer Gary saw repeatedly the mess caused by dysfunctional families and their kids and grand kids. He believes the Biblical family model is vital.

Unconscious Truckie Prostitute

The Great Western Highway in Sydney was a favourite spot for prostitutes, known as 'Truckies Moles' to sell their bodies to passing transport drivers both day and night. The truckies would stop, take the prostitute to a secluded spot and after a paid encounter drop them back to the highway. Sometimes after a dispute over money or services, the drivers were far from gentle, for they would push a prostitute out of their truck, sometimes even whilst it was in motion. Gary and his colleagues at Blacktown Police Station had carried out many law enforcement encounters against the prostitutes and their clients. High profile police cars were used to patrol the area.

One Saturday afternoon, Gary saw a prostitute on the south side of the Great Western Highway. He pulled up, told her to leave the highway and then continued his patrol. It was about 3 hours into Gary's shift when he was again patrolling the area and saw no prostitutes. As he arrived at the traffic lights at Reservoir Road, a man in a van blew his horn vigorously and waved his arm at Gary. The man yelled out, "There's someone lying in the grass about 100 feet behind you."

Gary gave the driver the thumbs up, switched on the lights on the top of the police car and carefully reversed up the road. Gary scanned the area but couldn't see anyone in the grass. He got out of the police car and walked to the top of the grassy embankment. From this vantage point he saw the prostitute he'd spoken to earlier. She was lying in the long grass.

Gary moved quickly and when he examined the girl, he discovered she was unconscious and did not respond to any verbal or painful stimuli. Gary saw fresh needle marks on the inside of her arm. An empty fresh syringe and needle were in the grass not far away. There were no obvious injuries on her.

Gary called for urgent ambulance assistance and placed her in the recovery position. The girl's breathing was failing rapidly. Gary got his resuscitation mask and quickly put on gloves as he thought CPR would be needed soon to keep her alive.

In no time, other police arrived with an ambulance. The ambulance paramedics examined the girl and said, "We'd better hurry. She's as flat as a tack." They inserted a cannula into the back of her hand and injected a good dose of Narcan, which is used to temporarily reverse the effect of the narcotic overdose on the brain.

The girl quickly became conscious and suddenly without warning she shrieked and pushed the paramedic away. She lunged underneath her dress with her hand, causing Gary to take urgent action. He reached past the paramedic and grabbed her hand and pulled it out from underneath her dress thinking that in her confusion, she was going for a weapon such as a knife, scissors or razor blade. Gary knew it was a custom for prostitutes to hide a small weapon in their panties in case of danger from a client or pimp.

The girl started to resist violently and still tried to get her hand under her dress to obtain a weapon. A serious struggle took place between the prostitute, Gary and the other police as they tried to prevent her becoming armed. Finally, they handcuffed her with her hands behind her back. She still struggled even with handcuffs on. She wriggled and tried to get her hands under her dress. Gary then became assertive and directed one of the paramedics to get the weapon while the police held the girl down.

The paramedic lifted the girl's dress and searched her panties. He was shocked. He looked at Gary and anxiously said, "Gaz, the reason she's screaming: she hasn't got a weapon in her panties but her genitals and anus are crawling with dozens and dozens of black bull ants. She's inundated with bites both internally and externally. They evidently crawled all over her while she lay unconscious in the long grass."

The paramedic said,"Quick, let's get her in the back of the ambulance."

The police lifted the girl to the ambulance. Paramedics washed and irrigated the infected areas as much as they could before urgently transporting the girl to Blacktown Hospital Emergency. She was still hysterical. She was immediately taken into the operating room where a consulting gynaecologist checked her out and removed the ants.

The next morning, Gary went to the hospital to interview the girl. Young as she was, Gary was surprised to discover she was married with two children. Her husband had left her for another woman and left her destitute. She's worked in a brothel at Doonside, became addicted to heroin and decided to prostitute herself on the Great Western Highway to get more money and try and avoid the pimps. She said she'd been bashed around, robbed, pushed out of trucks, all in a day's work. She said she used to earn the rent and her children's education but it all collapsed two years ago into her heroin addiction. Every cent she earned went on drugs. The Child Welfare Agency (DOCS) took her two boys and fostered them out. She said she's had enough of life and was on the brink of suicide. The overdose episode with the ant infestation in the long grass was the last straw.

Gary said, "I'm a Christian. Can I speak to you on a personal basis about your life?"

"Yes of course," she said with tears.

"All of these things you've just told me are going wrong in your life; God has an answer in Jesus."

"How?"

Gary explained the gospel to her. His heart broke for her and the mess she was in. So he prayed for her and when he'd finished, he opened his eyes to see her crying into the pillow.

She said, "I know you're right. You're not the first Christian to speak to me about Jesus. There's a Christian Street Team that comes around the streets giving us coffee and something to eat. They said to me many times, you need Jesus."

The girl went on to say, "After that episode yesterday, I can see now I do need Him. A social worker wants me to go into rehab with the Salvation Army."

Gary said, "Yes it's a great program. You didn't know this, but I go to the Salvation Army and often speak at their rehab meetings about being a Christian police officer. I trust I'll see you there."

Roughly three weeks later Gary spoke at the Salvo rehab meeting. He saw the girl there. She greeted him warmly with a hug and yelled out to all, "Here's the Sally Cop who saved my life. He used to be my cop, now he's my brother." Gary got a standing ovation from those who normally are angry with police.

This is one story that had a happy ending for she graduated, re-married, got her two boys back and is leading a fully committed Christian life. She has a job and is loving life.

Gary says, "What we muck up, God can fix up."

Thinking back, Gary was amazed at the way God showed him and the passing motorist where the girl was in the long grass. He realised that even a couple of minutes later she would have had a respiratory and cardiac arrest. It would have been extremely hard to save her life.

Gary notes that a part of Jesus dying on the Cross was to forgive our sin. The other part was to heal our lives. The episode highlighted the depth of degradation addiction can cause so Gary says to readers, "Don't ever experiment with or use unlawful drugs."

The Razor Gang

There were a couple of drug users, husband and wife who were shoplifting to support their habit. They kept stealing from retail stores. It was the task of the police to catch them. Gary says he looked at closed circuit television footage. The couple would stand in front of razor blade fixtures and stuff bulk packets of razor blades down the front of their clothing and then leave the store without paying. They kept stealing many packets of razor blades. A search warrant was organised for their home.

When the warrant was executed, the premises were searched and the police discovered the house was full of stolen goods. The most interesting thing was the fact there were hundreds and hundreds of razor blades they had stolen. It became quite a joke among the police. The couple were charged with numerous charges and they were nicknamed the 'Razor Gang'. They received about six months jail for their collection of stolen property. Happily, the whiskers of Australia are being shaved again.

On Not Being Camera Shy

On numerous occasions (far too many to mention) Gary carried out drug raids on premises. He says they looked for leaf, resin or plants growing. Often there were some complicated hydroponic set ups. They did a raid in Prospect. There were quite a number of mature plants worth $40,000 to $50,000 on the street. They were tall plants; they found bags of dry leaf and arrested four offenders.

One offender was not there at the time of the raid. He was arrested later. After a caution, Gary said to him, "Do you know anything about this plantation"?

"I don't know anything about it. I know nothing."

"We found your fingerprints on the hydroponic equipment."

"Oh, yes we were growing tomatoes."

Gary said, "Let me show you a photo."

Gary showed the man a photo of four blokes and said,

"Can you tell, me who this is in this photo?"

The colour drained from his face as he paused before he spoke. He said, "Obviously it's a photo of me."

He had his arm around one of the plants. He was cuddling his marijuana. Gary said, "What is that you have your arm around?

"It's grass, marijuana. I helped grow it."

Gary smiled, "It makes an interesting photo. I don't think you'll be leaving here?"

"No, I don't think I'll be leaving."

Gary charged all men with cannabis cultivation. They received hefty fines and a bond.

Gary points out offenders often take photos of themselves with drugs, weapons, stolen property or money. Often the police find photos of people posing with contraband. He says they once arrested a fellow for armed robbery. They found a photo of him in a bath with his girlfriend. They were bathing not in water, but with stolen money. They found another photo of him on the bed with his girlfriend. They were covered not with a blanket but with more stolen money.

Gary was able to enhance the photos and match the numbers on the notes with money taken from the bank during the hold-up. Gary points out that people take photos with mobile phones and upload them to Facebook, Twitter or load them onto computers. It's part of their gratification and showing off. They make a record of their criminal deeds. It's almost an addiction. That's why criminals take photos of themselves in various scenes: because they want to repeat the gratification. In addition, they want to be able to show others. It's attention-seeking behaviour or looking for approval. Police use these images and social media material as evidence for prosecutions.

The Man with the Iron Bar
At Blacktown, a tow truck driver had turned up to re-possess a car. The car's owner lost his temper and told the driver to go. The driver said, "I have a possession order here." The owner attacked the truck driver with an iron bar, hitting him on the head and shoulder. He then smashed every window in the tow truck. The tow truck driver was taken to hospital by ambulance with non-life threatening injuries. He later recovered after getting stiches in a head wound.

When police arrived to see what the row was about the car owner threatened them with the iron bar. Gary arrived on the scene. He stepped out of his police car and walked up the driveway. Police had their hands on their guns just in case the man attacked. Gary found the man yelling and screaming. He waved the iron bar above his head threatening police with death. His eyes were glazed and he breathed heavily.

Gary spoke to him softly but firmly, "Please put the bar down. We need to go to the police station and discuss what happened here today."

Gary thought to himself that there's more to this than meets the eye. Gary said to the man, "Demonic spirit, leave the man, in the name of Jesus."

The man stopped, stared at Gary, looked at the police officers, looked at the iron bar, threw it away, put his hands down and said, "Why are the police here? What have I done? I'm so sorry."

The man was told to lie down on the driveway. He complied. He said, "Please don't hurt me."

He was handcuffed, arrested and searched. He was crying as he was walked to a caged police vehicle. He pointed to Gary and said, "I want that man with me in the back of the truck to help me."

Gary said, "No, I can't do that, but I'll follow you to the police station."

Gary remembers as he drove behind the caged truck, the man's fingers were protruding out of the back door slats. At the police station Gary made a cup of tea for the man before charging him with malicious wounding and other offences. Bail was refused. Next morning at court, the Magistrate asked the defendant,

"Which solicitor is representing you?"

The accused said, "Mr Raymond is representing me."

"No, Mr Raymond is the police officer who arrested you. A solicitor must represent you."

"No. Mr Raymond has been very kind to me. I sacked the lawyer. Mr Raymond will help me."

"Mr Raymond can't carry out that role. You need a solicitor."

But Mr Raymond was good to me even though I did something very wrong."

"We'll have a short adjournment. Mr Raymond will explain to the defend ant what he needs please?"

"Yes Your Worship. I will."

Gary explained to the man what the system was. He eventually agreed to have a public solicitor represent him. The man later pleaded guilty and received a short jail term.

Gary noted how Jesus, as our prosecutor, became our defender.

Trapped by Lollies
There was a call over to the Westpoint Shopping Centre at Blacktown. There was a lolly machine where you drop in a coin,

turn a coin carrier and it drops a lolly down a chute. A boy about ten years of age tried to get a free lolly by sticking his fingers up the chute. The result was his two fingers got trapped in the machine. He and his mates tried to release his fingers but they failed. The security guards tried to get his fingers out by using liquid soap. At this time, not too many people noticed the drama being played out at the machine.

Since the security guards couldn't get the boy's fingers out. Next the Police Rescue Squad was called. Gary says when they arrived they had to dismantle the lolly machine bit by bit. When they took the bottom panel off, lollies came raining down and rolled all over the floor. Lollies went everywhere. By this time, there were about 300 people watching the drama and about half of these were kids. Naturally, as the lollies scattered everywhere the kids raced to grab as many as they could. One little boy filled every one of his pockets to overflowing with lollies and ran away. As he ran, his pants fell down around his ankles with the weight of the lollies and he tripped over, losing a lot of his stolen lollies. The other children screamed with laughter when they saw him. He quickly got up, pulled his pants up and this time held them as he escaped with his rather diminished sized loot.

Once gaining open access, the Rescue Squad used some lubricant and some strips of X-ray film which depressed the fingers slightly and allowed them to gently pull the fingers from the machine's chute. The Rescue Squad carry a special 'Finger Kit' which is especially designed to get people's fingers and toes out of difficult situations. It contains small tools for delicate and close quarter extrications.

With his sense of humour, Gary said jokingly to the boy whose fingers were trapped, "You'll have to pay for all the missing lollies, you know?" Gary felt a bit awkward because the boy started to cry. Gary apologised and reassured him it was only a joke. The Rescue Squad proceeded to assist centre management to pick up the lollies that hadn't been collected. They had to be thrown out for health reasons. The young fellow went off to hospital by ambulance for a check up because his fingers had been squashed in the coin mechanism. He only had minor injuries. He was left to steal lollies another day, or maybe not. Gary thinks the boy will think twice before he tries to get a free lolly from such a machine again.

A Dash without a Splash
There was a police random breath testing operation in Western Sydney. A vehicle failed to stop. When this happened, a Highway Patrol car and followed in pursuit. The pursuit went on for ten minutes or so. It was a safe pursuit. Many people do not realise there are strict rules for police pursuits. Police drivers are certified to take on pursuits. Drivers of such vehicles are skilled in pursuit. They give their classification, their experience over the radio. They also give the direction of travel, description of the vehicle and driver, road conditions, weather conditions, speed of the vehicle and manner of driving. While this is happening, a senior police officer and the Police VKG Radio Senior Operation Officer monitor the pursuit. Those listening will determine whether or not to terminate the pursuit.

Alternatively, the police driver himself can terminate the pursuit if it's dangerous. The police driver must also adhere to the Police Safe Driver Policy. Police drivers keep in mind that even though they are seeking to apprehend wrongdoers in such pursuits, it's still an offence for a police driver to drive at a speed or manner dangerous to the public. There is no open cheque to drive beyond your their own ability or risk management. It's not good to endanger those around.

So off they went in pursuit of the vehicle that didn't stop. The containment of an offender's vehicle (unlike America) is to never to create physical contact with the offender's vehicle. To force it off the road or into another vehicle and cause a collision is prohibited. Gary says this driver went into a suburban street, which was a dead end. He was by himself. The police car followed and contained him there.

The offender took off on foot up a driveway of a suburban house. He then jumped over a fence in the dark. Gary says the police ran up the driveway pursuing the man on foot. Gary had arrived also. Next, Gary heard a loud thud and then screaming. When they reached the fence, shone their torches over it, they saw the offender lying on the bottom of a swimming pool. The trouble was, when he jumped into the pool, he did not realise it had no water in it! He was at the bottom all right, on the concrete bottom!

The offender had multiple fractures. The ambulance and Police Rescue were called knowing the offender would have to be carefully lifted out of the pool on a special rescue stretcher. He was taken to hospital. It did not tak long to discover he'd been drinking. Blood samples were taken at hospital. He was later found to be two times over the limit. He was also unlicensed. As a result of his escapade, the man did community service, copped a heavy fine and licence suspension. Also he was in and out of hospital for about a year having the fractures fixed up. He had further surgery. He was left with a bit of a disability with his legs.

Gary points out, this is what people don't realise. In this case, the offender not only paid a fine, he also paid the price of having an injured body. He was unable to work while he was being rehabilitated. This is also a cost the community, a great deal of money. If he'd stopped at the RBT, he would have been tested, charged with drinking and driving, not having a licence and simply had a slap on the wrist. People fail to realise what they get themselves into when they try to evade an RBT testing station. Better still, don't ever drink and drive; it's the sensible way.

Grass Trap Door Dealers

An outlaw biker gang was suspected of dealing in drugs at a Doonside hotel. Gary was a detective and was put on the case. He'd done some initial surveillance, which wasn't successful. As a result, he had a bright idea: he went to a block of flats and asked an elderly couple if he could use their unit for covert surveillance. They agreed. It didn't take long for Gary and his partner to discover the drug dealers had a hole in the ground covered by a grass covered trapdoor. The drug dealers would put the drugs in the hole then close the trapdoor. The drug users would come along put their money on the dealer's table, open trapdoor, reach in, and get their marijuana wrapped in tin foil.

Gary took video and photos. One afternoon, he raided the hole and took possession of the drugs. He later arrested one of the key dealers who was the Sergeant At Arms of an outlaw biker club in the area. At the Police Station he cautioned the dealer and interviewed him. Gary said, "What can you tell me about the selling of marijuana at the Doonside Hotel on this date?"

He laughed, "You won't get me Mr Raymond. I was just having a beer."

"Do you want the good news or the bad news?"

"What do you mean?"

"Have a look at this. I've got you on tape and photographs dealing."

Gary showed him all the photographic evidence during the interview.

"So what, that doesn't prove much."

"Oh, another bit of bad news is, I've also got your fingerprints on the foil the drugs are wrapped in."

Gary showed him the statement from the fingerprint expert. He nearly fainted.

"You've got me Mr Raymond, you clever bastard."

Gary explained that crunched up foil was not easy to get fingerprints off, however this offender had wrapped the drugs up and twisted the ends of the foil, thus leaving his fingerprint on the body of the foil, which was still nice and smooth. It was a 'minor detail' overlooked by the offender, which ended in his demise. The drug dealer was charged with supply and pleaded guilty at court. He received 12 months jail and a heavy fine. It's a case of people not knowing these things. Traps for the unwary indeed.

TOP COP

The drug operation was closed down permanently by Gary and his team.

CHAPTER SEVEN
RAYMOND ON POLICING

"I want to go back to a time when I was very young, when you expected the police to be part of the community and the community to be part of policing." David Blunkett (British Member of Parliament)

"From a policing perspective our job is to gather evidence, analyse evidence and present evidence. What happens after that in the court system we cannot have any influence on." Wayne Oates (Psychologist)

What can you say about being a Christian in the Police Force?
Gary answers, "Being a Christian in the police force is exciting. We see a number of incidents in the Bible of policing. When the Romans invaded a community, they ceased to be soldiers and became like police officers. What do I mean? Well, they quashed riots, patrolled the streets, arrested thieves and murderers and helped collect taxes. The fighting on the battlefield stopped and they became law enforcement officers.

"There are of course a number of Roman Centurions mentioned in God's word. In one case (Luke 7:1-10) a Centurion with a sick servant sends a message and tells Jesus not to come to his house but just say the word and his servant would be healed." Jesus said of that Centurion, "I tell you, not even in Israel. Another case was at the cross have I found such faith." So this 'cop' had enormous faith that even Jesus talked about. When Jesus was being crucified, a Roman Centurion was also present at the cross. When he stood in front of the cross and watched Jesus die he said, "Truly this man was the Son of God." You see, one of the first to acknowledge the deity of Jesus Christ was a 'cop'. Given these cases, it's easy to be a Christian cop. Just have uncompromising faith and acknowledge Jesus as Lord, like these two 'cops'."

What are some traps in policing?
Gary says, "The question of reasonable force in arrests can be a difficult one. Reasonable force means using only enough force that is necessary to bring an offender under control. Once a suspect is restrained, police are not lawfully allowed to punish the offender with physical or mental violence. That's regarded as going overboard: like giving a few extra punches or excessive wrestle holds which may amount to 'torture'. If the offender is smaller than the police officer, that doesn't matter. They may be fuelled up on alcohol or drugs and have extra strength and mental drive which requires lots of force to restrain them, despite their size.

"Then again, if the offender is bigger than the police officer, more force may have to be used. Sometimes deadly force is necessary. The offender may draw a firearm or cutting weapon and a life-threatening situation arises. Police have to act and act quickly. Often an enquiry goes for weeks on a decision that went in seconds. Police are also entitled to defend themselves and anyone else whose life is threatened. In the event of a fatality, the State Coroner has jurisdiction over the matter. It's regarded as a 'death in custody'. It must always be born in mind, the sole purpose of the police is to arrest an offender and bring him or her before a court."

What about 'P' plate Drivers?
"Young people have to understand the psychology of risk taking behaviour. Why do they drive fast? Why do they lose control and take risks? Why do they race each other? It's certainly not the road

or the vehicle. We should not run driving courses but a course for young drivers on the reasons for risk-taking behaviours. Experts could explain what happens in the mind under peer pressure. Their self-esteem and competitive nature could be explained to understand the mental processes that happen when they decide to drive fast. Young passengers have a huge influence over young drivers as well. Someone in the car suggests they do some inappropriate behaviour and they do it. Why? It's not so much driving skills but behaviour control skills that need to be taught.

"In the course, there would be role-plays in the classroom. I suggest they put them in a mock car. Have other role-players act as passengers and other drivers egging them on to put their foot down. I believe that will help them understand what happens and give them practice on how to stay in control of the temptation to do stupid things with the car.

"Another thing I'd do is take them on a skid pan to show them what happens when the car is out of control. When you're out of control, nothing works. Part of the workshop would be to say 'It can happen to you'. I'd explain what happens when a car is out of control: they become a 'passenger' in the driver's seat of their own car. All these fancy driving schools don't explain what happens when you're out of control. Out of control really means 'out of control'. Look at Peter Brock, a most experienced driver. He was killed when the car was out of control. We need to reinforce if it can happen to him, what about us? Young people think it can't happen to them. Part of the workshop would be to convince them it can happen to you!

"If driving a car is something a person is going to do for the rest of their life and it's important they start their road sense education at an early age. There is really no age limit to start road safety education. The child's education on road rules should be done from the start. We take them at a young age to learn numeracy and literacy.

"Because it's such a responsible thing, there should be a Diploma in Driving. Learning to drive in different conditions, different roads, changing a tyre, basic mechanics, first aid and mental attitudes to driving and much more. I think it should be a diploma course rather than just driving around the block and then getting a driver's license.

"Most blame the young driver but the greatest risk is their passengers. The drivers often do what their passengers tell them to do because they don't want to be rejected by their peers. They look for approval and popularity from their friends so they do things to please the crowd. We have to teach passengers to be 'responsible' passengers. A car with teens stopped at lights. A car is along side with another bunch of teens. They harass the driver, 'Your car's better than his, drop one and drag him off'. Young drivers look for reputation. They have to learn to have the courage to say 'No' rather than just give in to their so-called friends. They have to earn a reputation for not dragging rather than dragging. It's a reversal. Defensive driving and road rage prevention should also be taught. Look at what they have to do to fly an airplane. I think that same level of instruction should be the same for a motor vehicle."

What causes the individual to speed?
"It's usually a lack of proper time management. It's all mental. They're angry because of their own inadequacies. Then again, impatience is the worst thing.

"A fellow came roaring past me in a vehicle on the Great Western Highway one night. I'm doing 80 kph, the speed limit, and he went past me like I was parked. I couldn't even get his number plate to notify police he was so fast. I saw him again at Red Rooster, Lithgow having a meal with his wife and two kids.

"I stopped and said to the man, "I'm Gary Raymond, a retired police officer. I need to talk to you about your speed and manner of driving."

"What is it got to do with you?"

"Just calm down mate. If you don't listen, I will phone the police, make a statement, have you booked and go to court as a witness. Which way do you want to do it?"

"Go ahead and say what you want to say."

"Do you agree you were well beyond the speed limit?"

"Yes I was."

Gary noticed his wife looked upset she said, "I've been begging him to slow down. He doesn't realise he puts me and the kids in danger. He is so impatient when he's driving." She began to cry.

The man said, "I'm very impatient on the road. I know I need to slow down. I get uptight."

Gary replied, "Maybe you might need some counselling to help that behaviour?"

"Yeah, it may help. I'm sorry mate. You're right, I was going too fast and I'm glad you're talking to me. I need to wake up to myself, a wakeup call."

"You can see mate, speeding didn't help. You stopped here for a meal and other cars have gone past you that you overtook up the road. You've gained nothing."

"I agree."

"If you keep speeding, one day your kids will be calling someone else 'Daddy' because you'll be dead or end up in jail."

He started to cry.

Gary said, "I didn't mean to upset you both. It's pointless speeding. You see trucks screaming down the road, stop at a truck stop, have a feed, shower then get into their sleeper cab and go to sleep. What's the point? You see motorcyclists taking a risk dodging between cars and then they're stopped at a red light. What's there to gain? Some years ago, we did an experiment with a police car going from Railway Square to Circular Quay with a siren and lights on. Then another police car did the same without lights and siren. There were only minutes between them. So please mate, you don't want to kill your wife and kids. Slow down. I hope our encounter today meant something. Thanks for listening and all the best."

"Thank you for going out of your way to have a go at me. It's just what I needed."

Gary shook their hands and continued his journey.

What comment can you make about safety and security in the community?
"Safety and security is vital for without it, nothing else in the community works. You can't do things in Syria in the centre of the fighting, because it's not safe. You can't drive to the hospital because it's not safe. You can't have a business because it's not safe. Everything else is underpinned by law enforcement. We need more police. Some say the police should work harder or smarter but no, the need is for greater numbers."

An empty park.
"A youth leader in one of the churches planned to hold a youth concert in a big public park. The purpose of the night was to gather a whole lot of young people together to hear music and good speakers. Gary and a former heroin dealer, who had become a Christian, were to speak. They were to talk about their Christian lives. Gary went to the park. There was a stage, lighting and sound system set up ready to go. When Gary arrived, he noticed there were no young people.

About ten minutes before starting time, four young people, two male and two female came and sat in the middle of the Park. It was hoped a thousand would come. The time to start came and went but no more young people arrived. The band was all ready. The youth leader came up to Gary and said,

"This is a flop Gaz. Sorry about this. We'll cancel it."

He walked away to speak to someone else.

Suddenly, God the Holy Spirit said to Gary in his heart,

"This is not a flop. You need to do what Jesus called you to do. Jesus met with one woman at the well and you're complaining about four young people in a park."

With a tear in his eye, Gary muttered, "Sorry Lord, please forgive my ignorance."

Gary went to the organiser and said, "God told me that if Jesus could spend time with one woman at a well, we should speak to four kids in a park. Jesus was not a 'numbers' man. He was concerned with quality not quality. On occasions He spoke to 5,000 plus people and one also woman at a well."

The organiser told the team what God had said to Gary. The team went to the back of the stage, knelt down and prayed asking the Lord to forgive them for having such shallow faith. Gary said, "Let's go. Put the night on." The four young people stayed. No one else came even whilst the music was underway.

The former drug dealer spoke, then Gary spoke. At the end, they asked people to come forward and confess Christ. Each one of the four young people came forward separately and surrendered to Christ. It could be honestly said that one hundred per cent of the audience came forward and made a decision to follow Jesus that night. The night was over; the youth leader was full of joy that those young people made a commitment. The young people disappeared into the night. Everything was packed up and the park was back to normal.

Some years later, Gary was speaking at a church gathering at North Sydney. The assistant pastor went up to him and said, "I've met you before."

"Where?"

"Remember the youth meeting in the park at Ashfield? I was one of the young people who came forward at the appeal that night. You'll be delighted to know the other three are involved in fulltime Christian ministry right now."

Gary was overcome by emotion as he flashbacked on that night that nearly didn't go ahead.

Gary points out, "Ours is to sow the seed and not to always look for fruit. We must trust God. Go by faith, not sight and he says of God, "My ways are higher than your ways. My thoughts are higher than your thoughts."

"God is involved in multiplication. Who knows how many have been won into the Kingdom of God by these four young people?"

Gary, how do you view Capital Punishment?
"I don't agree with capital punishment. The biblical principle reveals two types of justice: God's justice and justice here on earth. We can't always trust the courts to get it right. We see people acquitted who were found guilty and jailed. Even today, innocent people are executed around the world. I don't think you ever get the real truth of a crime sometimes if there is complicity in one person and not in another. Is there a category of sin? No, sin is sin. No degrees of sin, but there are degrees of consequences. Remember our Lord told us, "Let he who is without sin cast the first stone." Remember self righteousness is a mankind thing, not a God thing, whether an offender or a victim. I trust God's justice, not mankind's."

A Word on Victims
"Victims of crime can go through a critical incident stress. They go through enormous trauma. Few people really understand the trauma for victims of crimes. Watchers of television mostly treat it as fantasy. Just another news story. This problem is also heightened when there is threat of death or serious injury to someone, better know as a 'near miss'. The emotional stress around a sexual assault or robbery victim is high. Feelings run all over the place. Victims often fantasise over what they did or didn't do. What we call the 'what ifs'. For instance, 'I shouldn't have gone through the park at night'. This is part of the grief. The best support is just being there, sitting with the victim, listening. This helps them deal with guilt and regrets."

CHAPTER EIGHT

RED FOR DANGER

"To a profound pessimist about life being in danger is not depressing." *F. Scott Fitzgerald*

Fire at Luna Park
On June 9 1979, seven people died when a fire engulfed a ride at Sydney's Luna Park. Jennifer Poidevin lost her husband and two young sons. She said, "Strange how things turn out. It was a Saturday and two of our teenage children planned to visit Luna Park 'just for fun' as the advert said." What was to be a night of family fun for many who attended Luna Park became a parent's worst nightmare?

A fire broke out on the Ghost Train ride. The ride was made up of open carriages on tracks like a small train which made its way through dark timber constructed tunnels, containing scary images, noises and ghost like figures. Microphones throughout the tunnel amplified peoples' voices as they screamed at the startling sights and sounds.

Seven people died in the fire: a father, his two boys and four of their classmates.

Gary says, "I'd been on the Ghost Train in the past on a visit to Luna Park. On the fateful night, Gary and the Police Rescue Squad were called by the fire brigade.

Gary said, "When we arrived the area was well alight. It was an extremely hot fire. We were told there were still carriages inside the tunnel. To make matters worse, there were still people trapped inside. Since it was of wooden construction, the flames had quickly taken hold and engulfed the whole Ghost Train system. The tunnels gave the fire lots of oxygen as the air rushed through pushed by air pressure. The night sky was a bright orange glow with smoke pouring upwards. Lots of hot embers streamed upwards through the smoke.

"When the fire was extinguished, a search for bodies began. The grey ash from burnt timber was deep. We used wire coat hangers strung together to form a probe. We had to prod the ash to find people. You knew the difference between the ground and a body. The bodies were soft when you found one with the probe. We also probed around to find any belongings that might have survived the fire. It was a most distressing operation. We also had to locate evidence and the origin of the fire.

"The odd thing I noticed was the silence. Normally there are people screaming with laughter on the ride. It was surely a place where the lack of sound after the fire really hit you. There were smells for sure: burnt wood smells, the smell of timber. The smell of humans who had lost their lives pervaded our nostrils. When we found the bodies, they were charred and unrecognisable as people. It is very difficult to get them into body bags and onto stretchers. A very difficult task for all involved.

"A man came up to me. He was cuddling his two kids. They were all crying. He said, "I was just about to put my two kids on the ride. I couldn't because it was full. So we went to another ride. We watched them carry bodies to the ambulances. I imagined my sons being carried away and realised it was someone else's children." It was horrible."

Gary explained, "All of us in the fire brigade, ambulance and rescue squad felt the tragedy deeply. A coronial inquest was unable to establish the cause of the fire, but concluded that Luna Park's managers and operators had failed in their duty of care towards the park's patrons. The fire forced the closure of Luna Park until 1982, when it reopened under a new name and new owners."

Bomb at the Hilton Hotel

If there's one thing in Australia's history that causes controversy whenever it's discussed, it's the Hilton Bombing on 13th February 1978. Three people were killed: one police officer and two garbage collectors. The bomb was planted in a rubbish bin and exploded when the bin was emptied into a garbage truck outside the hotel at 12:40am. It killed two garbage collectors, Alec Carter and William Favell. A police officer guarding the entrance to the hotel lounge, Paul Birmistriw, died later. It also injured eleven others. Police officer Terry Griffith was seriously injured by flying shrapnel. He still suffers with his injuries today.

Twelve foreign leaders were staying in the hotel at the time, but none of them were injured. Australian Prime Minister Malcolm Fraser immediately called out the Australian Army for the remainder of the CHOGRM (Commonwealth Heads of Government) meeting. The intriguing thing about the bombing is that even to this day the perpetrators remain unknown. Arrests were made but this did not clarify the situation. It appeared that this was an attack on the Indian Prime Minister. It was certainly a terrorist attack and a rude awakening for Australia. Most of the world leaders were in their pyjamas and were led out to safety. The bomb had been placed in a garbage bin. Unsuspecting garbage men had disturbed the device probably by the truck's compactor.

The bomb exploded outside the Hilton Hotel in the heart of Sydney. Names swirled around, all finally to no great affect. Informants there were and evidence was muddled until in the end no one really knew exactly what happened about the planning and reason for the bomb, except that three people were killed. The situation was well summed up on the 25th Anniversary of the Bombing, in an article entitled, Lies, spies and the Sydney Hilton Bombing: -

Who planted the bomb that killed two garbage men and a police officer? The courts jailed the wrong man and after years of false imprisonment, Tim Anderson was set free. Evan Pederick, who said he did it and offered himself up for jail, later said perhaps he was mistaken about his confession and now is studying to be a Church of England priest. Police, who were shown to have falsely claimed they arrested men with a bomb, kept their jobs, their bravery medals, their promotion and their salary increases. Did Amanda Marga do it? Was this the first case of political terrorism in Australia? Some people say that Police Special Branch or ASIO (Australia's Security Intelligence Service) did it for political purposes. Can we ever name the Hilton bomber(s)?

Gary Raymond was called to the scene and I'll let him tell his side of the story:

"A call came through to the Rescue Squad. A bomb had gone off in the city of Sydney. We were in disbelief. We immediately thought it must be a gas explosion and someone had it wrong; maybe an electrical fault had done it. In those days the word 'terrorism' was hardly used. Not like today were terrorism is everywhere. We discovered it was an Improvised Explosive Device (IED). When we arrived in George Street, we saw there was debris widespread.

"There was shrapnel everywhere. Worse still, there were body parts everywhere. We sadly discovered they belonged to two garbage men. I found two spinal columns with bits of pelvis and skull attached on the road behind the garbage truck. I found other body parts in windows, on awnings and on the roadway itself. It was so bad we had to 'grid' the body parts where we found them. Limbs had even been blasted into shops. We had to photograph and tag the body parts before they could be sent to the Sydney mortuary. My brother Neil was at the scene since he was attached to the Police Forensic Services. He was involved in the investigation and Disaster Victim Identification (DVI)."

The Scar-Faced Kidnapper

A young fellow in his early 20's was severely burnt during an incident. The fire left him with a badly scarred face. Due to this event he went through surgery and therapy. The result was he did not feel anywhere near normal. He believed no woman would even look at him and this played on his emotions.

One night he stalked a young girl who was taking dancing lessons in Blacktown. He had a fixation on her, which led to the stalking. One night as she walked along a street in Blacktown, he followed her in his car. He then made a rash decision to abduct her. He drove his car beside her, jumped out and forcefully dragged her into the car with the aim of sexually assaulting her.

Because of the scarring, he thought he could never have a meaningful relationship with a woman unless he forced her. This led to the criminal fixation on the young girl. When he got the girl into the car, he drove around at high speed trying to find a suitable location. He wore what looked like a bandage wrapped around his face to cover the scars. He wore this on a permanent basis. The girl, full of terror, thought he was going to kill her so she looked for an opportunity to get out of the car. But because of the way he was driving, she couldn't find an opportunity. She looked for a red light hoping he would have to stop. With no red light in view, she realised there was only one-way to escape, and that was to jump out of the car. She waited until the car slowed down on a bend on one of the outlying roads in the western suburbs of Sydney. As the car reached an intersection and the driver turned the wheels, she was released from his grip. She opened the car door, threw herself out into the road and ran to the nearest house. The youth stopped the car, but when he saw her run to a house, he sped off.

People in the house rang the police. As a result, uniformed police arrived and took down details. Gary, as the on duty detective was handed the case to investigate. The girl had minor injuries as the result of her jump from the car. After being treated in hospital, the girl was interviewed and the police were able to get a description of the offender and his car. At first, the police thought the bandage was a type of disguise.

They then asked questions around the streets of Blacktown. Then a call came through to the police station at Blacktown. It was from a young woman who said she knew a young fellow who wore a bandage around his face. She provided a name. Police enquiries led them to where the youth lived. He was there with his bandaged face. He was arrested and his car was confiscated for forensic examination. He did not admit anything during the interview. At that time, the police were not sure they had the right person. As a result, that night the police conducted forensic enquiries. They found a number of light coloured hairs in the suspect's car which matched the hair of the victim. When confronted with these facts the youth couldn't explain. Finally, he confessed he was the offender. He was subsequently charged with abduction, false imprisonment and assault.

After the interview, Gary talked to the youth about his life. He asked, "What's wrong with you? Why did you do this to the young girl?"

The young man told him, "I'm ugly. My life's worth nothing."

"You might be ugly on the outside but if you come to Jesus and ask Him to take away your sin, your ugliness will be overcome by the beauty of Christ. Let the beauty of Jesus be seen in you."

He said, "People will always see me as ugly."

"Would you rather be seen as what people see or what God sees? If you trust in Jesus people will see the difference."

"How do I do that?"

"You just ask God to forgive you. You'll be clean and all the inside scars in your spirit will be taken away."

At this point, he started to cry. Then he said, "I want that to happen."

He prayed a simple prayer, asking God to forgive him, especially for the offence for which he'd been arrested. He received Christ as his personal Saviour. He received many years in prison for abducting the girl.

Some years later, Gary was speaking at a large church gathering. He told those present how it's possible to be a police officer and a Christian at the same time. He told the story of how Christ changed a young fellow who had a badly scarred face;

how the young man became beautiful on the inside and how God sees us, not how we see ourselves.

After Gary finished speaking, a lady stood up in the middle of the congregation and said, "I'm sorry to interrupt Mr Raymond, but that young man you just spoke about is my son." Then, pointing to a lady beside her, she said, "This is his grandmother. When we visited my son in prison, he told of a police officer who arrested him and led him to Christ. I'm so pleased. I've been waiting to meet you for years and to thank you for what you did on the day you arrested him. He's a new person and always says he's not beautiful on the outside but he's beautiful in Jesus on the inside."

At that moment, the whole congregation broke into applause. It was a very moving moment. The grandmother sat with tears streaming down her face. After the service, Gary was able to speak with the two ladies over a cup of tea. It is proof God can change even the 'ugliest' lives.

Danger in Court
Gary happened to be present at the Blacktown Courthouse on another matter when a man was brought up from the cells on drug dealing and drug using charges. Gary noticed the man looked very angry and stressed out. He was probably withdrawing from drugs. There certainly was no mistaking the fact of this man's anger when he started grinding his teeth. Gary only had to look at the eyes, the windows of his soul, to know without any shadow of a doubt, he was burning inside with resentment.

The facts of the case were read out. Immediately the man stood up in a rage and yelled, "It's not my fault I'm a raging junkie. I need help. Won't someone help? All you want to do is to let me rot in jail." He became abusive and swore uncontrollably. Police officers started to approach him to calm him down. Without warning, he suddenly jumped from the dock holding area and ran past the bar table. The magistrate, terrified, rose from his chair and ran to his chambers and locked the door. This is common practice when a critical incident arises in the courtroom.

The man grabbed a pen from the table, held it in his fist and moved it backwards and forwards in a knife-like gesture. Fear gripped the people in the court. Solicitors and court staff ran for their lives. Gary and the other police could see that this was a dangerous situation and withdrew to a safe distance. Gary put his hand out in a friendship gesture and started talking to the man calmly. He said, "What are you thinking right now mate? Why are you here doing this?"

The man screamed, "I'm not going to jail. Over my dead body I'm going back to jail. I'm not a violent person, but I'll kill myself before I go to jail. I'll put this pen through my eye into my brain if anyone comes close to me. Do you hear? I will, I promise you."

"Please don't do that mate. Promise me you won't stab yourself in the eye."

"No, I can't promise you. I just want all this to end."

"You say you're not a violent person, but you're threatening to gouge your eye out and you're threatening us. What does that say? Please don't get violent. How do you know you're going to jail? Your lawyer will examine the case and present it to court. Trust your lawyer. What if you suicide and you weren't going to jail after all? What a waste. Your life is worth more than that. Just calm down, put the pen down and let the court deal with your case in a fair way.

"Killing yourself is a permanent solution to a temporary problem. We can get you to hospital and into a drug detox unit. Would that help? Look mate, to be straight, God has a good plan for your life just give Him a chance. Let Him help you through this. Just put the pen down and start again."

Then Gary said," I'm going to pray with you."

Gary closed his eyes and prayed that God would give the man a real peace and a trust in his future." When Gary opened his eyes the man was crying and staring at the pen in his hand. He walked over to the table, put the pen down and walked back into the prisoner dock holding area. Gary and police approached and handcuffed him. He was still crying and began apologising. The magistrate adjourned the case and ordered the man be transported to the Blacktown Hospital for medical and psychiatric assessment.

The man was so pleased he was getting help and said to Gary, "You are my saviour."

Gary replied sincerely, I'm not your saviour mate, but I know your real Saviour, His name is Jesus. You need to surrender your life to Him. As I told you, He has a plan."

Asian Drug Dealers
Gary was appointed to Cabramatta as an Acting Inspector, Duty Officer. Gary thought getting into gang investigation work would be very interesting. He'd done Christian Street Team work and was used to street gangs and the drug scene, both on and off duty. However, he got a shock to see the extent of drug dealing in Cabramatta. Gary discovered Vietnamese and Cambodian gangs were dealing in the CBD and east-side of Cabramatta. He was also surprised at the type of dealing.

The dealers held drugs in small balloons in their mouths. They would place them under the tongue so if police encountered them, they'd swallow the balloons and drink copious amounts of water. When police left, the dealers would ram their fingers down their throat and vomit up the balloons. Others would collect the balloons in their faeces, wash them and sell them. Initially, the police would sneak up on them, grab them by the throat so they couldn't swallow and make them spit the balloons out. An Ombudsman complained and the police weren't allowed to grab drug dealers by the throat anymore. They had to go gently, gently.

At one stage, the heroin dried up due to the Americans in Afghanistan destroying the opium poppy crops in a bid to stop money going to the Taliban terrorists. Much of the opium crops stopped producing. The majority of drugs were brought in to Australia via the post, airport and wharfs. Tighter border security meant drug couriers (mules) found it harder to smuggle drugs into Australia. The increased search of personal property and cargo entering our ports slowed the spread of the drug trade. Despite all those measures, lots of heroin still entered Australia, especially Cabramatta. Whenever the heroin came directly onto the street, there was always a massive increase in overdoses, keeping the ambulance and police busy.

Gary attended a traffic collision where a school boy was knocked off his pushbike. When searching the boy's backpack for identification, Gary found a large amount of heroin. Gary found $300 in the boy's wallet. Gary later found out that the Vietnamese 5T Gang were using school kids to run drugs from one part of Cabramatta to another on pushbike or on foot. The kids that did this made much more money as drug couriers than newspaper delivery boys. The drug dealers would even send kids onto school buses or trains to see if the other kids wanted heroin. The police in many ways were handicapped for they could only give a youth caution to those they caught.

Dealers would also use 'stand-over' tactics and force shop owners to hide drugs for them. The dealers would threaten to beat up a shopkeeper or they would have his shop burnt down if he didn't conform to the demand. Dealers would walk into the shop with an empty bag and walk out with a bag full of apples, oranges and drugs. Melons would also be cut open, drugs placed inside and the melon super glued closed.

They would also threaten elderly people and make them carry drugs from one end of the main street in Cabramatta to the other. They also dealt in pension protection. This meant if you carry these drugs, your pension would be safe. Otherwise they would assault and rob them of their pension money as payback.

On one occasion, Gary says they'd been told a couple had bought heroin. There was a thorough search but no heroin was found. Gary called in a police drug dog. When it arrived, it gave a strong indication after it smelt a baby in a pram. Where were the drugs? Much to his horror, Gary discovered four balloons of heroin inside the baby's nappy. The couple were arrested and Community Services were called in to take care of the baby. It was a sad affair where even babies got chosen as drug couriers.

The dealers were crafty indeed. They would lease a series of units throughout Cabramatta and would hop from one unit to another to keep on the move. They had no furniture and slept on the floor. The units were just used for dealing or injecting heroin. These became 'stopping' places for dealers and druggies alike.

Back in those days, the cost of a small heroin balloon was between $20 and $30. It was a huge business. Gary says they could pull up a drug dealer and find he was carrying between $5,000 and $7,000 from a morning's work. When asked, "Where did you get the money from?" The answer was invariably, "Gambling," or "I loaned money to a friend and he's just paid me back." Gangs would open or take over restaurants, then they would go and have a meal and buy heroin at the same time. Next, they would shoot up in the toilets. Gary found a restaurant on the east side that had no food or chef. The ovens and deep fryers were stone cold. The restaurants were purely a 'front' for the sake of appearance. In the same way, they would open up a snooker room. They would have heroin in packets taped to the underside of the table. Gary even found heroin hidden in a 'hollowed out' pool cue.

There were many stabbings with cutting weapons when dealers clashed with other dealers or drug users. Rip-offs were common. A person in debt to dealers was in a very dangerous position. Prostitution, robbery, theft and other crime was used to pay back debts. Stand-over tactics were common. Machetes were a favourite weapon. Gary sometimes found guns, swords, martial arts weapons, daggers and flick knives on suspects. The police were given the power to search people suspected of carrying knives unlawfully. There were hefty fines ($500) for carrying knives. However, there was so much money flowing around because of the drug trade, the fines did not seem to worry the dealers.

The dealers were getting tired of getting caught with knives so they started hiding their knives under garbage bins, in trees, drain pipes, gutters, electricity boxes, phone boxes and many more 'hidey-holes'. On occasions they would run into a restaurant's kitchen and take a knife from the chef to fight with. Some would bandage or tape a knife to their back, thigh or buttocks. This meant the number of knives being carried around Cabramatta trebled. When trouble started, they would go to a knife hidey-hole and get one to use, then put it back. As a result, there was many nasty stabbing and slashing cases.

In such a competitive environment with the constant struggle for power, one can see how it was not strange someone like the late Member of Parliament John Newman could get assassinated. He was a strong fighter against the drug trade, but no match for a bullet.

On one occasion, Gary had a search warrant for a dealer's premises. He went to a unit with other police. The drug dealer fled over the balcony into an adjoining unit. He came out the front door into the stair well. Gary reached the stairs below him. Suddenly, he produced a long machete, raised it above his head, and threatened Gary and the other officers. Gary tried to negotiate. The man threatened to cut Gary's head off. A dangerous situation indeed, Gary removed his pistol, pointed it at the man and said, "Put the machete down now; put your open hands above your head now."

The reason for hands above the head was some of these offenders put small razor blades or flick-knives in their hair, beards, taped on necks or shoulders. Police don't say, "Put your hands on your head" for that reason.

The man refused Gary's demand. He started to slowly walk down the stairway towards Gary. Gary quickly pulled out his capsicum spray (CS) and fired four bursts of spray directly at the man's face. The man was of Asian descent and had a turned up nose. The stream of CS spray went straight up his nostrils, in his eyes and over his face. He screamed uncontrollably, dropped the machete and fell down the stairs, narrowly missing Gary and other police. The machete clattered down the stairs after him and was recovered by police. He was writhing with discomfort on the landing below. He was subsequently arrested and handcuffed. Back at Cabramatta Police Station, an ambulance was called to decontaminate the suspect.

The ambulance officer said, "Where's is it hurting?"

The man cried out, still shrieking, "Please help me. It feels like my nose has blown open and my head has been blown off. My face is on fire and I can't open my eyes."

The ambulance officer smiled and used some liquids and cleaned him up. Gary looked at the man and said, "Feel better now, I hope? It's better you get some capsicum spray than a bullet from my Glock (police issue pistol). You are a very fortunate man that you weren't shot." The man was convicted of drug offences, assault and many more. He received 9 months in jail.

It's all in the Understanding

It was a special day at Cabramatta Police Station. Japanese police officers were visiting Sydney on a study tour. Gary travelled to the city and accompanied the 15 Japanese police to Cabramatta. There was an English language interpreter with them. One of the Japanese police sergeants said, "We think it's disgusting that you have so many prostitutes on the streets here in Sydney. We would never allow that in Japan."

Gary didn't know what he meant and asked him clarifying questions. Again he repeated, "We think it's disgusting that you have so many prostitutes on the streets here in Sydney. We would never allow that in Japan."

Gary asked him to point them out, which he did. Gary laughed his head off and realised the Japanese officers didn't realise they were not prostitutes, but office girls who'd come out of their offices downstairs onto the street for a smoke break. After the explanation they all laughed. Apparently, the girls were leaning around on buildings, with handbags over their shoulders, smoking cigarettes, looking like 'call-girls'. Gary laughed and told them, "Gentlemen, I assure you everything in Australia has an explanation."

Gary showed these officers from Japan around Cabramatta in a mini bus. As part of the tour, he showed them a public toilet in the BKK car park where drug users congregate to inject. He explained the drug trade and drug use. At one stage, Gary looked near a toilet door. To his surprise, he saw four feet. Looking under the door Gary saw two men unconscious. He also saw a needle and syringe on the floor indicating they had probably overdosed. Gary broke the door down, pulled the men out and called for ambulance and police back up. The Japanese police (like tourists) went into a frenzy and started snapping dozens of photos.

When two young Constables arrived they started physically pushing the 'photographers' out of the toilet block. They thought they were all local Cabramatta residents who were interfering with a police operation. That was until Gary yelled, "It's okay guys, they're with me. They're Japanese police."

Back came the reply, "Oops, sorry boss." The Constables apologised. The Japanese smiled and bowed. The Constables bowed. The bowing seemed to go on and on. Then the photo frenzy started again when the ambulances arrived and performed their treatment on the overdoses.

The day was full of dramatic police work. The visitors saw, and of course photographed, arrests, vehicle crashes, overdoses, stabbings and assaults. Gary took them to a famous John Street restaurant where they enjoyed a genuine Vietnamese noodle soup. They left to go back to the city. Gary estimates they took about 500 photos each. True story.

Gun out of a Window

Gary was working at Cabramatta. He was on a routine foot patrol with a female police officer and they were not far from the CBD. At the time there was a great deal of drug dealing, drug carrying and drug using going on. Gary was the Duty Officer that day. The two officers were keeping their eyes on things. Gary remembered the words of the late Sergeant Ray Tyson of the Police Rescue

Squad, who used to say, "Always look up, down and around you constantly." People who didn't want to be found would be seen—in a tree for instance. This Gary did as a matter of habit.

This time as he looked up, he saw the barrel of a rifle poked out of a window of a block of units. Gary did a rapid 'double take'. At that moment, he did not know if he and the female police officer were the targets of the gunman. Gary flew into action. He lunged sideways and knocked the female police officer over a brick wall and held her down behind the wall as she said, "What's up boss? What's up? What's happening?"

As they settled on the ground Gary said, "Be quiet. Bang stick third floor." 'Bang stick' being police slang for gun. As Gary held the female officer down he said, "Stay down." Gary crawled along the grass to see what he could find out. The rifle was still sticking out of the window. Gary urgently called on his radio and told despatch they had an offender with a firearm and an unknown description of the offender and gun.

Gary also told them to approach from the northern end so they would have adequate cover behind the units. Gary and his female partner stayed down behind the wall, with their guns drawn, to give themselves cover. After all, they still did not know if they were the ones targeted and could have been shot if they left their safety cover. The unit number was established. The police formed a perimeter to contain the gunman in the unit. The gun was withdrawn.

Police crept up the unit stairs and carefully evacuated the other units. Gary and his partner stayed under cover. The State Protection Group arrived and called on the suspect to come out with hands up and leave the weapon in the unit. This was done on a public address system. The police had people who spoke various languages so the order was given in Vietnamese, Cambodian and Laotian. Gary told his partner that they would stay in position until the situation was secure. It took a long time before the offender was flushed out, a matter of hours. Finally, the offender came out of the unit hands high above the head.

A police dog was sent in. The dog found another offender who was hidden in a cupboard and was flushed out. Gary and his partner left their cover. A search warrant was applied for and granted. Gary says they always ask for a search warrant for a gun and parts thereof. He says that if you are looking for a rifle, you cannot look in a drawer but if it's for parts thereof, you can. When the police went in, they found an unloaded rifle with telescopic sight.

A search of the premises was carried out. One weapon was found, but they couldn't find any extra bullets. Gary told the search team search again. They said they'd done a good search. Nevertheless, Gary insisted on another search. One sharp young officer found some bullets in the toilet bowl. The offender had tried to flush the ammunition down the toilet, without success.

One of the suspects admitted the gun was his. He said he was pointing it out the window because his mate wanted him to shoot some flying foxes. Their intention was to cook and eat them. He said they were a delicacy in Asia. Unfortunately, they did not seem to realize, as Gary pointed out, that the flying fox community at Cabramatta River were a protected species.

Gary was in the unit as the police completed the search warrant. He looked out a window and noticed that right opposite the unit was a snooker room, which was reputed to also be a gambling den. Gary had a hunch. He went over to the snooker room and asked the owner, "Do you know a man by the name of........."

He said, "Yes we know this man, he works for another bad man who collects gambling debts." He pointed at a man across the room. Gary approached him and asked, "Do you know.........?"

"Yes, I lost a lot of money from gambling and last night he threatened to kill me, shoot me. His boss said that if I didn't pay, he would have me killed. Why do you ask?"

It dawned on Gary what was probably happening. The man at the window with the rifle may have been involved in a contract killing arrangement. Gary put the facts together.

Gary continued, "The man I mentioned was in that unit over there and had a gun pointing over here. I think he planned to kill you." At this, the targeted man got very angry. Gary thought that this is good, for he might be able to get him to make a statement, which he did.

The detectives took over the case because of its seriousness. However, all the witnesses that had been spoken to withdrew their statements in fear of reprisals from the 5T gang. The police had to let the offender go after he was charged with a number of firearm offences.

Witnesses dropped off because they were scared of the 5T gang. It's worth noting the 5T gang came into being as a result of youths who came to Australia with their parents after the collapse of the Republic of Vietnam. Many of the families who escaped from Vietnam settled in the Cabramatta area. By the mid 1980s, a group of youths gathered and formed the 5T gang. Supposedly, 5T stands for Jail, Death, Guilt, Love and Money, since the words for each of these words starts with T in Vietnamese.

An alternative meaning was that the five words were 'Young People Lack Of Love.' Members of the gang had a tattoo. This consisted of a straight horizontal line and 5T joined vertical lines. The head of the group was a youth by the name of Tri Minh Tran. In 1989, he was only 14 years of age. Born in Vietnam in 1975, he was seven when his parents brought him to Australia. It did not take him long to turn to a life of crime, for when he was eleven years old police arrested him for carrying a sawn off shot gun. Within two years, he was suspected of murdering two rival gang members.

It didn't take long for 5T to get involved in the heroin trade. "Criminal gangs in the Vietnamese community are increasingly heavily armed, are moving into drugs and gambling, establishing links with Australian crime figures and becoming involved in stand-over rackets in their own community." *(Sydney Morning Herald January 1988)*

Many warnings about the danger of the 5T gang were given.

One advocate for dealing with them was New South Wales Member of Parliament John Newman. Unfortunately, he was assassinated and his voice was no longer heard. His view was that youths belonging to the 5T gang should be dealt with by sending them back to the jungles of Vietnam where he said they belonged. He knew this was something they feared most of all. Yes, they could injure, maim and kill, but to be sent back to Vietnam that was something else.

It was after the death of John Newman that public attention was drawn to the 5T gang. Then in 1995, Tri Minh Tran and his second in command were murdered in an apartment at Cabramatta. A power struggle followed. This resulted in another leader being killed. Violence escalated as rival gangs struggled to dominate. There was an enquiry in 2001. At the enquiry a police officer by the name of Tim Priest, who was based at Cabramatta at the time, warned there was a rise in gang violence. Reba Meagher, John Newman's successor as State Member for Cabramatta, criticised Priest and called him a 'disgruntled detective'. John Aquilina, New South Wales Minister for Education at the time, forced her to apologise. Rightly so.

Gary says the biggest challenge for police in dealing serious crime is with witnesses. Witnesses often don't come to court or forget vital evidence whilst in court. On occasions, they abuse the Witness Protection Program by making unfair demands of the police. They can say if you don't listen to my demands, I won't stay in the program. Often, they slip surveillance and go back to their area, get some drugs and then come back to their supposedly-protected hiding place. Gary points out, it's very hard to deal with protected witnesses, especially over a long period of time. Gary says, "In regard to the gun out of the window case, that's one of the frustrations of witnesses not having the courage to give a statement and give evidence in court. Crooks get away with it and live to cheat, threaten or kill another day."

Finally, with extra funding and resources, the police got the upper hand in Cabramatta and the names of gangs such as 5T,

Four Aces, Madonna's Mob, Black and Red Dragon finally faded into oblivion. Cabramatta today is a safe, vibrant suburb, well worth a visit to its Asian restaurants, fabric shops and markets.

A French Stabber

Gary was at home when a call came through to say there was a double fatality over a cliff at Manly. A car had gone over a footpath on the southern end of Manly Beach. When Gary arrived, a Detective Inspector told him there were two bodies in the vehicle. But this was no ordinary road crash.

Forensics had discovered the dead driver had a knife in his hand and a dead woman front seat passenger had multiple stab wounds to her chest. A bystander said the driver had driven straight over the footpath and through the fence and over the cliff at high speed. The identification found they were both French citizens. The next day the autopsies confirmed the male had stabbed the female several times in the chest at the same time as he drove the car at accelerated speed over the cliff. The knife had been bought at a hardware store by the driver that day. It still had the bar code and sticker attached. Enquiries through French police tracked the dead man's parents and the dead woman's mother in France. In time, they also found her father. Then the sad story emerged.

They were boyfriend and girlfriend in France. The relationship failed and the girl tried to stay away from him. The man had started to stalk her in France and tried to take control of her. She came to Australia to get some breathing space away from him. That didn't stop her boyfriend locating her and flying to Sydney. A friend told police, the man rung his girlfriend and told her he'd come all the way to Australia see her to tidy things up. He told her wanted to have a last meal to finish the friendship up and he would return to France and not see her again. He needed closure, not a sudden separation. She thought that would be alright; she would just meet him and close the relationship. It seemed a reasonable request and after all, he'd come across the world.

The man picked her up that night. They had a nice meal at Manly. Police found out the knife had been picked up that day. It was clear he intended to kill her if she ended the relationship. The driver's parents came out from France and also the girl's mother. Then detectives were able to get more details from the parents.

After the investigation was completed, the bodies were released and placed in the hands of the French Authorities and each placed in sealed coffins for the journey back to France. Gary went to the airport to see the parents off. They thanked Gary and his team for what they had done during the investigation. Gary said, "It's ironic they were apart in life but now their bodies are together in the cargo hold of a jet in death. Sad for both families. No one wins. Domestic violence is serious. Victims of threats, stalking or control should take it seriously and seek law enforcement advice and counselling before it's too late."

Drop the Gun

It was a summer's night. Gary was on duty with a detective mate, having a general walk around the Blacktown CBD and railway station. There had been complaints about drug dealing so he was on the watch out for anything suspicious. However, all was quiet.

Suddenly the night air was pierced by a man yelling and a woman screaming. The stress was coming from the vicinity of the night chemist shop. Gary and his mate ran across the road to the chemist and his assistant. Just at that moment, Gary saw a man wearing a balaclava and carrying gun running east in Main Street.

The chemist yelled, "We've just been robbed."

Gary and his mate ran after the robber. He turned right into Flushcombe Road. Gary and his partner were catching up. They drew their .38 Smith and Wesson police revolvers. The robber turned right into a laneway at the old Blacktown Post Office. Gary and his mate followed. As they rounded a corner running, they were presented with the greatest shock of their lives. The robber stood in the middle of the lane with a gun pointed straight at Gary and his mate.

Gary says, "We had been taught in officer survival training never to run or look around corners as you didn't know what was around the other side. What did we do? We ran around the corner right into the barrel of a pistol. It was like a movie or nightmare. You go into disbelief, but thankfully I took action. I knew that most gunshots to the chest were fatal. I dove to my left into the gutter to protect my chest. I knew I might survive a headshot, even though I would not be in a good condition. I pointed my gun at the robber's chest and screamed at him the drop the gun now. My mate instinctively dived into a shop alcove, which was to his right. Not good cover but better than nothing. He pointed his gun as well and yelled on the robber to drop the gun.

"I started to pull the trigger of my revolver and the hammer started to come back. In other words, I was ready to shoot and kill. So was my mate."

Thankfully, the robber dropped his gun and put his hands up. Perhaps the shock of us both yelling at the same time caused the robber to drop his gun. The robber cried out in a panicked voice, "Don't shoot, don't shoot, and whatever you do, don't shoot!"

Gary and his mate eased off the trigger pressure. They were only a 'touch' from pulling the trigger to fire off shots. Talk about a close call. You don't get any closer than that!

Gary yelled, "Keep your hands up."

The man went down on the ground with his hands out front of his head as Gary's mate put his foot on the man's back. Gary handcuffed him. He then took off the robber's balaclava. What was the next big surprise? The robber was only a 14 year old boy!

Was there yet another big surprise?

Gary then went over to the gun and picked it up. He nearly fainted. He realised it was only a toy plastic gun like the ones you get at a two dollar shop for your kids to play with! Gary told his mate and they shook their heads in disbelief. What a sigh of relief they didn't shoot him.

Looking back, in the dark, the plastic gun looked like a real automatic pistol. The offender was searched. The stolen money was discovered in his pocket. In such a case, the money was counted, serial numbers noted and used as evidence.

As Gary recalls the incident he says, "We really thought for sure he was going to shoot us. I think if the gun had been real, we may have died, if we didn't get him first. There was only limited fluorescent street lighting. Imagine the newspaper headlines next day:

Cops shoot 14 year old kid carrying a toy gun
Gary says, "The sad fact is we have the dilemma facing all police. It's not what they think at the time of the incident and the risks involved, but how the courts will see the incident three years later. As in many cases, the police face a harsh review of their actions or inactions in a critical incident. Hindsight is easy. Will the court really understand what they went through or other cops in similar situations? Criminals always have the advantage for if they're armed and dangerous they will always shoot on sight. Whereas the police always have to consider the risks involved in making the wrong decision. One has only to consider recent events as presented by the media where the police are all too easily accused of being overzealous."

Gary and his mate rang the young robber's parents to attend the station for the interview. They refused and told Gary 'where to go' in no uncertain manner. They've had enough of their young drug addict son and were emotionally unable to support him anymore. Gary got a Salvation Army Officer to attend the station to sit in on the interview. When the official interview was over, Gary had a conversation with the young robber.

"Mate, I just want you to know that we nearly killed you tonight. I want you to know that death is permanent, not like you see on the movies or computer games. Your body dies but your spirit, that is you personally, goes on to heaven or hell. Do you see how serious it was tonight?"

"Yes I do, but things are going wrong 'cause I'm on drugs and desperate."

RED FOR DANGER

"I am a Christian and I know God has a plan for you mate. I reckon God was in that laneway tonight and actually saved your life for a purpose. Why don't you get detox and rehab?"

"I want to but they said I'm too young."

"No way, I can get you into a special youth program if you want to do it." After tonight you have to realise God is giving you a second chance at life."

"Yes, I'll do it," was the reply.

"You know mate, Jesus died to forgive us all and that includes you. You have to go to Children's Court for the hold-up and probably get detention but, if you surrender your life to Jesus, you'll be free within yourself and have a new direction. What do you reckon?"

"Yes, I want Jesus."

Gary prayed with the lad and so did the Salvation Army Officer. The lad ended up in tears and realised he needed drastic change, the type of change only God can give. He received a remand to go to rehab, which he did successfully over nine months. When he went back to court, the character references were so glowing, the Children's Court Magistrate gave no detention, just a good behaviour bond for 1 year. The young man completed an Electrician's Trade Course and is married with a two sons. He attends church regularly and helps with the youth group. He contacts Gary from time to time to catch up. They are always reminiscing how God saved his life in that laneway years earlier and brought Gary into his life to hear the wonderful gospel message.

Gary, with a tear in his eye, says, "You see the Bible is right: In Christ you can become a new creation. The old goes and the new comes (2 Corinthians 5:17). The foulest can become clean. Thank you Lord for renewing many lives like mine and my young mate."

CHAPTER NINE

A TOUCH OF HUMOUR

"Humour is mankind's greatest blessing." *Mark Twain*

A Truck Duck

Gary had been seconded to Building Industry Task Force, attached to the Gyles Royal Commission. On his first day back in uniform at Blacktown he was assigned to general duties. It was quite a transition from plain clothes to uniform. However, Gary took it all n his stride. Gary was working with a female officer on the caged police truck answering emergency calls and other types of police work. A call came in: a drunk was directing traffic in the middle of Richmond Road, Blacktown, causing chaos. Gary was on the way.

As they drove over Railway Bridge on Richmond Road they saw a big white duck running around in circles on the road. The duck had probably fallen off a poultry truck on the way to market from one of the many farms at Schofields. They saw it in the middle of the road with traffic stopped to avoid hitting it. Gary chased the duck around the bridge to everyone's amusement. He finally caught it and boy, did it put up a fight. Gary finally threw it into the back of the police truck, with the loud applause from the delayed motorists. Gary laughed and said, "No Facebook or Twitter in those days, thank goodness, otherwise we would be famous!"

He told his partner that they would take the duck to the Featherdale Wildlife Park. Just as that decision was made, another call came in via Police Radio Centre that the drunken man was directing traffic, becoming more aggressive and threatening motorists. Gary realised that that had to get the bloke first. They arrived and the man aggressively approached Gary. Gary swung him around and placed his arm up his back. His partner handcuffed him. He struggled and swore his head off. He was placed in the rear of the caged truck.... Yes, with the 'angry' duck!

Gary said, "They made a good pair; both had failed the 'attitude test'. They began their journey to the station. Then all 'hell' broke loose in the back of the truck. The duck started to vigorously flap its wings, jump up and down and peck the drunk at every opportunity. He was trying desperately to push the crazed duck away with his feet but that caused the duck to peck his feet and legs even more intently. The man complained bitterly through the observation hole to the driver's cabin.

"I yelled out that we would be at the station in a few minutes. The duck continued its defence after being caged up with such a 'crazy' man. I told my partner to make it quick back to the station, otherwise we'll have a full blown riot in the back. She put her foot down. We didn't know whether to laugh or cry."

At the station, Gary and his partner brushed all the white feathers off the stressed drunk. He was then taken inside and placed in the prisoner's holding dock. The Custody Sergeant came in. He was a very popular character, a very hard man with a sense of humour, and very sarcastic. He ran a tight ship. He said to Gary, "Pray tell Mr Raymond, what is this gentleman to be charged with?"

Gary was just about to answer when the drunk piped up loudly.

"Ah! You mate with the three stripes. I've got a complaint about these two idiots" (pointing to Gary and his partner)."

"Are you referring to me and my two fine colleagues?" Gary asked. "By the way, I don't believe I'm a mate of yours, so don't address me as one."

"There was a big white duck in the back of their truck attacking me. Look at me, scratched everywhere. They put me in the back with a mongrel duck."

"I see Sir, you're telling me there was a big white duck in the back of the police truck. Is that right Sir?"

"That's right. I had to defend myself from it."

The Sergeant called Gary and his partner to an adjourning room.

"Gary I think this man has been on drugs as well as his alcohol. He's hallucinating. I think he needs to go to the hospital. He definitely has a mental health issue happening." Gary and his partner looked at each other and nodded their heads.

Gary said with a 'sheepish' look on his face, "Serg, there is a big white duck in the back of our truck."

There was a pause.

"Oh okay, it looks like you two need treatment at the mental health unit, as well as him! Pray tell, please explain Mr Raymond."

Gary explained the situation. The Sergeant shook his head in disbelief, had a sigh of relief that there was a plausible explanation, although not happy with Gary and his partner. The Sergeant said, "The duck must be thirsty. Bring it in here for a drink. I'll put our mate in the cell to sleep it off."

Gary brought the duck inside. It was a lot calmer outside of the confined space with a drunk. It was quacking and wiggling its tail. It drank water and had a nibble of corn from someone's lunch box. All of the staff came down to see the special prisoner. The Sergeant knew how to pay Gary and his partner back. He made Gary and his partner hold the duck up and placed the Prisoner Name Identification Board at the front of them whilst many photos were taken of the prisoner and 'arresting police'. It was even considered to take 'foot' prints to identify the duck in the future! Everything was going well until the 'prisoner' started to drop sloppy and smelly 'messages' all over the Sergeant's custody area. Gary was quickly told to get that duck out of there and take it to the wildlife park, which he did.

On their return, Gary and his partner had the task of cleaning the back of the truck plus the custody area of the duck's leftover 'messages'. All in a day's police work, Gary doesn't think! Later that evening, the drunk was brought from the cell a lot more sober than before. He said to the Sergeant, "Where did I get these scratches?"

"You may have had a fight with a big white duck?"

"You know funny you say that, I had thought I had a dream about a duck?"

"Yes, the 'grog' gives you weird dreams. Off you go home, have a good night and thanks for staying at my motel," remarked the Sergeant, keeping a straight face.

Abseiling to Inspector
Back in his early police years, the Police Rescue was stationed at the Police Academy, Redfern. The Rescue Squad was on the ground floor and the 21 Division Special Squad was on the 1st floor above them. Practical jokes were part of the stress relief in policing. It gave light relief to cops and gave them a funny side of a serious day.

The Detective Inspector started to throw lighted firecrackers down over the heads of the rescue squad men as a joke. They would be checking some equipment, then 'bang', off would go a firecracker, frightening the life out of them. This went on for a couple of days with the young detectives upstairs fully supporting their boss's antics with raucous laughter.

Gary's Sergeant, the late Bill Fahey said to his men, "I've had enough of these antics from upstairs. We'll fix him once and for all." Bill came up with a payback. Pointing to Gary and another couple of young rescue men Bill cleverly schemed, "You blokes tie ropes off the roof and abseil down to his window. Lock off and throw some firecrackers through the window into his office. Then slide down to the ground, take off and hide. Sound good?" All of the boys laughed and were more than willing to do the 'commando' raid.

The day came for the 'incursion.' Bill found out the Inspector was in their meal room with his men having coffee. Gary and his mates snuck up to the roof, secured their ropes, clipped into their descending devices and at Bill's signal, leapt backwards over the side. They slide down the rope silently and stopped at the Inspector's office window, lit their crackers and threw them into his office. They swiftly slid to the ground, unclipped off the rope and ran inside the rescue squad and sat having coffee. Other rescue men quickly removed their ropes and hid them.

Next thing, bang, bang bang, bang; it sounded like a machine gun! The rescue guys covered their mouths and laughed quietly. Shortly after the 'raid', the Detective Inspector came down laughing and said, "Ok Sergeant, where are the men who threw fire crackers into my office?"

"Sorry Sir, I don't know what you're talking about. We heard some bangs somewhere but can't help you any further. Why, what's happened?"

Everyone burst into laughter. The Inspector, cracking up said, "You got me a good one Bill. The crackers went off on my desk and burnt holes in some of my files. How am I going to explain the blackened papers to the Detective Superintendent downtown?"

"I'm not sure Sir, but I'm sure you and your fine young, clever detectives will find a way. Are you planning anymore attacks on my men Sir?"

"No Mr Fahey, I think we'll call a truce and have a beer tonight at the Clevo." (the infamous Cleveland Inn Hotel). The truce was kept and lots of laughter after work at the Clevo. However, the Inspector never did explain how he covered the 'black holes' in his files. It is a trade secret, no doubt.

On Going Through the Roof
The Drug Squad from the CIB, Gary and his team of detectives obtained a Supreme Court Warrant to install some listening devices in the home of a major drug dealer in Blacktown. They

were able to line up the specialist electronics police to install devices in the home of the drug dealer. Over two weeks, the police took particular note of the movements of the occupants of the premises, looking for a time when none would be at home. This was done by covert surveillance of the home and following the occupants day and night.

The detectives picked the right time and the right day when no one would be on the premises so that they could install the devices. They were all prepared and went out to the premises. They used radio contact and the State Protection Group in hiding to cover police in case anyone returned to the house. Two technicians climbed over the fence of the premises. They took a ladder and put it against a sidewall. The technicians were going to lift tiles, enter the roof space then put listening devices in the roof, then leave the same way. The two devices were quickly placed in the ceiling. Then as everyone was ready to leave the premises, there was an urgent call on the radio, "Abort, abort, abort." This was a pre-arranged signal if something went wrong to get out of there. They all 'took off like rockets' and met at the Blacktown Detective's Office. The technicians were covered in white powder.

Gary asked what happened. One of the officers said, "We were in the roof space when one of the ceiling beams gave away. We smashed through the gyprock and fell down into the lounge room of the premises. We weren't injured, thank goodness, but we realised there would be a lot to explain when the owner arrived home. I got onto his shoulders and retrieved the listening devices. We exited through the front door and here we are. Don't worry; it has happened before to some of our guys!" There was hysterical laughter amongst all the detectives.

Gary found out the owner came home and reported a break and enter offence at his home. The owner couldn't work out why nothing was stolen. The uniformed police took the call, attended the premises and made a 'crime' report. There was no forensic evidence found. It was later explained on the reporting system and withdrawn as a crime. Gary said it took another seven or eight weeks to get the listening devices installed. The same two police finally managed to get the listening devices into the roof of the house without falling through the ceiling again. "A great achievement," Gary suggests with laughter. The offender was finally arrested, with two associates for conspiracy to import heroin. They received lengthy jail terms. Gary said, "If things can go wrong, they will go wrong on police operations. There're stressful at the time, but later give us a good laugh."

The Black Plastic Caper
The Police Rescue Squad was part of the operational plans to attend siege, hostage, barricade or suicide situations alongside the State Protection Group (SPG). Gary and the Rescue Squad were involved in a training session with the SPG at night. They were testing a whole range of Rescue Squad spot and flood lights in armed situations. The idea was to set up lights on tripods in the dark, around a building where an armed offender was holding up. SPG operatives and snipers would get into position in the dark. Then at the right time, all of the lights would be switched on, blinding the offender and allowing the hidden SPG to engage.

The Late Sergeant Bill Fahey said to Gary, "I'll give you a slow whistle and that will be the signal for you to switch on the lights."

"Ok Bill," said a confident Gary Raymond.

All was well. The team operation was doing to plan. They were all set up. Gary heard a low whistle. Gary switched all the lights on. It looked like a Hollywood set or a football stadium. The only trouble was, the entire SPG team, yes all of them, had not yet got into position and were all exposed in the bright lights for the would-be gunman!

Bill shouted out, "Not now Gaz, you bonehead!"

Nearby there was a small roll of black plastic. Bill grabbed it and clipped Gary across the back of the head as he said, "Switch those blinking lights out, you'll get us all killed." Gary switched them all off immediately.

Gary retorted, "But Bill you whistled."

Bill was cranky. "I didn't whistle; that was a bird up there in that tree behind you. You should be able to tell the difference between my whistle and a bird by now. How long have we been working together?"

The Operation's Commander was also cranky.

He said, "Hope you're happy, Gaz. Whose side are you on? Most of my team are dead, wiped out in the wonderful light you provided. Thanks."

Gary was most embarrassed. They tried it again and this time Gary got it right. At the debriefing there was lots of laughter. Gary got a standing ovation for getting it right the second time. They never allowed Gary to forget his folly. Gary said, "I should have joined a Bird Watching Club to get to know the difference between Bill and the birds! I certainly got to know the difference, to avoid the 'black plastic'!"

It became a traditional saying in the Rescue Squad; if someone did something wrong, someone would say, "Get out the black plastic". For sure, Gary never lived it down, but all was taken in good fun. Often humour among members of the Rescue Squad saved the day in tense situations, and there were many.

Ladder to a Toilet
Gary went out with the Police Rescue Squad to assist 21 Special Squad to raid a gambling den in Surry Hills. Gary took a long ladder and had to wear dark blue overalls. Gary and his team snuck up to the building, on foot, in the dim light of an alley. He placed it at the toilet's fully open window and climbed up the ladder to the second floor. The plan was for Gary to get into the toilet, then run into the main gambling room and remove the front door railway sleeper that was keeping the door secure, before the bouncers realised what was happening. The rest of the police would then enter the front door to execute the Search Warrant.

At the toilet window, Gary turned around on the ladder and

A TOUCH OF HUMOUR

backed through the window down onto a toilet. Next minute there was a hellishly loud scream. Gary realised there was a man sitting on the same toilet that he had lowered himself onto. Gary got an equally bad fright as the man. Gary found himself sitting on the man's lap facing him. They were both in horror.

Gary stood up and, pointing his finger at the man forcefully, but quietly, said, "Police. I'm a police officer. Just keep quiet. This is a police raid." Gary showed him his ID & police badge.

"If you make a noise or move, you'll be interfering with a police operation, and that is a serious offence. Stay right where you are. Don't move. Do you understand that?"

The man, now pale, wide-eyed and shaking said, "Yes, Sir."

Gary peeped out the toilet door. The coast was clear. He then ran like mad toward the main entrance door, lifted the railway sleeper off the front door brackets, and threw it on the floor in front of the two 'man mountain' bouncers. They froze and were trying to work out in their mind what was suddenly going on. They call it the 'FFF: Fight, Flight or Freeze'. Thankfully for Gary, these two froze! Gary flung the doors open. In poured the police, mostly detectives. They corralled all the people on the premises, photographing and collecting exhibits. It took about an hour to complete the arrests and search. A row of caged trucks took the gamblers to Central Police Station to be charged.

As the police were getting ready to leave, it dawned on Gary the man was still in the toilet. He told one of the Sergeants how he stepped in on a man as he entered the toilet. They had a good laugh. The Sergeant then said, "Has anyone checked the toilet?"

"No I don't I think so," came the reply.

"Go and get him, Gary. I think I'll let him go after the trauma he's been through with you landing on his lap, two storeys up!"

Gary entered the toilet. Much to his surprise, the man was still sitting on the toilet, shaking. Gary said, "Come on mate, you can leave and go home. The Sergeant's giving you a break."

With quivering lips he asked, "Can I wipe my bum first please, Sir?"

"Yes, of course you can. Tidy yourself up and get out of here."

Gary waited outside and the man came out, looking around in fear. Down the stairs he went, never to be seen again in those premises.

Gary said to me, laughing, "Two things came out of this: that bloke would now always check to see toilet windows were shut and locked. And I now always check before I get off a ladder!"

CHAPTER TEN

A PRESENT HELP

"We can't help everyone, but everyone can help someone."
Ronald Reagan

A Nephew Rescued
It was a pleasant day for a family outing. Present were Gary, wife Michelle, Gary's mother, father, second brother Neil, wife Marilyn, and their children Patricia and Shane. They came down to Sydney from Newcastle to spend time with Gary and Michelle.

Gary says, "We went to Darling Harbour and entered the top outside deck of the Darling Harbour building. We were looking at the magnificent views of the harbour over the railing. There were vertical wire strands with stainless steel upright supports acting as a fence in those days. The lower strand of wire was about 40 to 50 centimetres above the floor level.

"As we looked at the water, someone said, "Where's Shane"? I looked around and couldn't see him. To my horror, with other family members, I saw two little hands holding the lower stand of wire. I also saw about half his forearms over the edge. Shane was gripping the wire strand and fully dangling his body over the edge above the concrete below! I'm talking about the distance of a one building storey drop.

"I believe now, because of God's help and my Rescue Squad experience, I was able to quickly lunge toward Shane very quietly but decisively and tightly grab his wrists. As soon as I grabbed his wrists, he let go of the wire. If I didn't have hold of his wrists, he would have plunged to his death or serious injury on the concrete below. I pulled him upwards and backwards by his wrists between the wire and onto the deck, landing him so that he was sitting him on his bottom. I stood him up. I was shaking like a leaf. Blood had drained from my face. We were all in deep shock. Shane's mother and father chastised him, but he was too young to realise the grave danger he was in. We all got emotional.

"The thing that saved him was the fact when I first saw him I was able to grab him. The others saved him too by not yelling out or screaming. If they yelled, I'm sure it would have shocked him and he would have let go. Thank God no one startled him. It saved his life. A great deal of my reflex action was due to the fact I learned about dealing with potential suicides when I was in the in the Rescue Squad. We learned about negotiating with people who threatened to jump from a cliff or building. When the time was right, we'd make a leap and grab the person dragging them back from the edge. It was instinctive."

One thing the Rescue Squad taught Gary was to be ready for anything. His many experiences added to his ability to save his nephew's life. God had a plan for Shane. Gary was so proud when Shane followed in the footsteps of his Uncle Bill, Gary, Neil and Kevin, who had all become police officers. Shane is a fine policeman who has saved many lives, himself being on the frontline of law enforcement.

Dragging a Girl off Rail Tracks
It was a hot summer's Saturday afternoon in Cabramatta. Gary was getting a few police together to check on drug users. They'd check the railway station first up. Gary at the time was working by himself as Duty Officer and went to the station to check it out before the other police arrived. He walked the platform closest to the CBD. A number of people were on the platform and people in the waiting room. Gary saw many of them were drug users.

A PRESENT HELP

They would buy drugs, shoot up and get the next train out of Cabramatta. The train had many names, including the 'White Powder Express'. Many users were on the nod (sleepy) after shooting up in the toilets or waiting room.

Gary turned to walk back to the ticket barrier when he heard a high-pitched scream, which startled him. He turned and went back to the platform. He saw a group of people at a spot down at the southern end. He noticed an old man yelling and pointing to the tracks. Gary ran to the end of the platform. He saw a young girl lying on the sleepers between the tracks. She was moaning and very distressed, and in a lot of pain. Because Gary had been talking to the Stationmaster, he knew a train was due. Without hesitation, he jumped down onto the railway line. He was breathing heavy, looking out for trains.

The girl said, "What happened?"

Gary said, "Don't worry about what happened. Hurry, get up."

"I can't, I've hurt my ankle."

Gary looked up and saw a train coming. In a panic, he quickly scooped the girl up with his right hand under her thighs and the other hand behind her back. He unceremoniously lifted her onto the platform, dumped her and rolled her to safety. Some people grabbed her and lifted her onto a seat.

In more panic now, Gary threw his leg up and pulled himself onto the platform rolling away from the edge. A couple of blokes dragged him clear of the edge of the platform. He heard the screech of train brakes with the train whistle blasting at the same time. This startled Gary and everybody else. People screamed. The train came to a stop halfway up the platform past Gary.

The guard then came up the platform and asked what had happened. Gary explained to him what had just occurred and radioed for an ambulance. The girl had had an overdose of heroin. She'd actually fallen asleep standing on the platform and fallen on to the railway track. She'd broken her ankle. The ambulance officers put a split on her ankle and gave her Narcan to reverse the effects of the heroin overdose.

People who stood by said, "You nearly got killed you silly woman. That police officer saved your life". The girl gurgled, "Ugh." Sadly, her brain was so saturated with narcotics she was in another world. She won't remember her close call, even to this day. Gary had a cup of coffee with railway staff to settle down before going about his business again. For Gary, it was another time he knew God's presence was helping.

The Roof Wrestle
A call came through for the police to go to a factory in Erskineville, Sydney where there were often break-ins. In this case, two men were involved in the break-in. One had given himself up to police, the other stayed on the roof. Police called him to come down. He simply abused the police and started throwing building materials down on them. The Police Rescue Squad was called. As a result, Gary climbed quietly up onto the roof opposite where the offender was abusing the police. Gary snuck around to the other side where the offender was. Gary heard a noise and realised the man had spotted him. The offender was agitated and walking around on the roof, with no disregard to his personal safety. Gary called out, "Give yourself up mate. Stop prancing around. You'll end up falling. Keep still."

"I'm not going down you'll have to come and get me," was the reply.

"You can't stay up here forever."

"Yes I can."

Gary suddenly heard another noise and quickly discovered it was the crash, crash, crash of the man's feet hitting the galvanised roof as he ran straight towards Gary. The man charged at Gary and tried to tackle him. He stood up and grabbed Gary's throat and tried to strangle him. Gary forcefully brought his hands upwards and disengaged the man's hands from his throat. They both started to wrestle and slipped down the roof to the gutter. Gary reached out and put the heel of his police boot in the gutter, acting as a wedge to stop them from falling.

Gary was now fighting for his life. It was clear the man was trying to kill Gary. He tried to get the man off him. Gary pushed one arm off and then the other. They were rolling around. The man was beside him. At this time, the two men were two storeys high above the ground. Using all of his strength, Gary gave him a swift powerful upper cut to the point of the jaw. Gary felt a crunch and was sure he fractured the suspect's jaw. This rendered him unconscious. Gary dragged the 'dead weight' body back up to the roof's apex. He handcuffed the man and put him in the recovery position. He searched him and found no weapons. Gary was exhausted and thanked God for saving his life. It was one of the closest calls he'd ever had.

At this time Sergeants Fahey and Beecroft arrived, came onto the roof and assisted Gary to lower the man in a harness off the roof to the waiting arms of other police. An ambulance took him to Royal Prince Alfred Hospital with a police escort. His jaw was broken in two places and was surgically wired up. He was charged with a number of offences and was given a jail sentence.

As Gary reflected on the incident, he said at the time he thought that if they'd fallen from the roof, he'd hoped he would land on top of the offender rather than underneath him. Gary also thought he might have used his gun and realised that if it had come to the pinch, he may have had to shoot him.

One thing Gary did say was, "Thank God for strong gutters."

He also observed it was a dry night. One could well imagine what might have happened had it been raining. It was discovered the offender was on drugs and alcohol, which explained why Gary had such a hard time trying to deal with him and get him to leave the roof. Yet another miracle from God's hand to Gary and his offender.

On Taking the Heat

There was a dangerous incident at the Paper Mills in Matraville. A worker was cleaning out a coal hopper container near the furnace. The coal went from the hopper, down a chute to feed the furnace's fire. The heat is used in paper manufacturing. A worker failed to put on his safety harness and while he was cleaning out the hopper, the coal collapsed, dragging him head first into the chute at the open entrance to the furnace. He was jammed in the chute with the coal. His mates could not release him. As a result, they rang triple 0. The call then went out to the Police Rescue Squad. Gary went with the Squad to the scene of the incident.

Gary says the heat was unbearable. The furnace was about 1200 degrees centigrade. It was like standing too close to a large bonfire and having to move back from the heat. Only on this occasion, Gary couldn't move back. Gary said, "That was a big difference from when I was working at the Thredbo landslide disaster. That was minus 9 degrees centigrade."

Gary and the team got to work very quickly as they knew the survival time in these circumstances would be low. They knew he'd become hypothermic and finding it difficult to breath. In other words, he was suffering Heat Stroke. Gary was lowered in a harness on a large rope from the roof to beside the chute. His task was to undo the bolts that held the chute in place on the hopper so it could be lowered to the ground with the man still inside. The squad would then cut the chute open and release the worker. Gary went down amid tremendous radiant heat from the furnace. He was using self-contained breathing apparatus but the air in the cylinders was becoming heated, causing him to inhale hot air into his lungs. He was sweating like he was in a sauna. He had no choice. It was urgent; no time for comfort.

He undid all the bolts but one. He struggled to get more energy. Gary realised he was overheating. The last bolt continued to cause him great difficulty. In his mask, Gary screamed out to God to give him the strength to undo this one remaining bolt. He grunted and put all of his remaining strength into the bolt. God gave him the strength. He undid the last bolt. He dropped the shifter and was lowered to the ground alongside the chute. Gary was seriously dehydrated. He couldn't even stand up and had to get help to sit on a box. After resting, he then drunk 'gallons' of water.

A PRESENT HELP

Sergeant Beecroft and the squad used an abrasive saw to urgently cut open the chute. Unfortunately, the man Gary tried to rescue was found dead. The ambulance crew attempted resuscitation but it was too late. At the time, Gary and the squad had presumed the worker was alive, until told otherwise. Gary and the squad slowly recovered from their exhaustion. While most rescues bring joy, this was one that cut to the heart. Gary was moved emotionally that in spite of all he did and suffered, he was unable to save the man in the chute. Gary was later told by the pathologist who conducted the autopsy on the worker's body that he was dead with 10 minutes of being sucked into the chute. It was long before Gary arrived. He rested in the fact he did all that he could humanly do, as always.

Glass Crate Rescue
A man was trapped by fallen pallets of glass. As a result the Rescue Squad was called to a warehouse, near Sydney. Gary discovered the glass sheets had been transferred by forklift. The vehicle came to a sudden halt and the glass sheets fell forward onto one of the workers. When the glass hit the ground some sheets became dislodged and shards of glass stuck in the workers skin impaling him. It was as if he was impaled on a 'bed of nails'. Gary said they put blocks under the pallets to stop the glass going any deeper. Because the shards were cutting into the skin, they couldn't move them sideways, for they would have caused serious injury to the impaled man. He was pinned face down.

The man was in considerable pain, with the ambulance crew on hand to help him deal with it. The police on site had to carefully crawl underneath the pallets and had to use hand tools to cut or break each glass shard and remove it from the man's skin until they were free to move him out from under the pallets. Ambulance crew directed Gary to remove the shards, as they would take the worker to hospital to have wounds irrigated and sutured. There must have been 20 or 30 glass shards. They then placed the man on a patient lifting board and slid him out from under the pallet where he was taken to the ambulance.

Gary pointed out that in rescue situations sometimes you have to remove the patient from the entrapment or the entrapment from the patient, or a little of both. In this case, the man had to have quite a few sutures. He recovered well and went back to work. Workcover carried out an investigation into the incident.

A Sad Arrest
It was a Saturday afternoon and all was quiet. Gary was in his Detective's Office at Blacktown Police Station catching up with some paperwork. He watched a footy match on TV in the background. A Detective from Balmain marched in with a young woman who was crying bitterly. He threw a bag of white powder onto the desk and said, "Gaz, charge this bitch with possession of this smack (heroin)."

Gary replied with indignity, "She's your prisoner mate, you do it."

"No Gaz, it's my own daughter."

Gary got a shock.

"Oh, sorry mate, I didn't know. I can help."

"I found her in the Prospect Caravan Park, Gaz, with this heroin in her possession, living with a heap of scumbags. She's badly addicted. I want her in court so she can be referred to a rehab program."

Gary made them both a cup of coffee. The girl said nothing. She was placed in an interview room. Gary did the charge sheet and obtained a statement from the Detective. When Gary was doing the paperwork, he asked the Detective his daughter's eye colour and date of birth. The Detective couldn't remember either of them. He began to cry. Then he said he couldn't remember but added with a questioning voice, "Hazel, I think they're hazel, Gaz?"

Gary pondered. Here was a father, a detective, who couldn't even remember his own daughter's date of her birth and eye colour. He reason was to follow. He had set up his garage at home into a study and went a long way in his academic studies. He spent hours gaining an advanced education. He admitted neglecting his wife and children in an effort to get to the top with police promotions. What sadness we find in the strangest of places. Truly, Gary was ready to help but in this case, the best he could do was to make a cup of coffee for two 'strangers'. Eventually, his daughter was clear of drugs. He abandoned his university study. The whole family reconciled and got their priorities straight. Gary was thrilled. Another mess turned into a miracle.

Wrap Up

The end of series two stories from the life of Gary Raymond has been finally reached. This however is not the end of the stories that can be told about this unusual 'emergency man'. Yes, there's more and the next series of stories are already being gathered together for you to read. It's a case of 'watch this space'.

A CHRISTIAN POLICEMAN'S PRAYER

Dear God, please help me to be your hands, feet and voice wherever the call of police work takes me. Help me to remember I'm one of your ambassadors and like the ambassador who represents his or her country, I'm on duty 24 hours a day. I must always be aware I wear the badge of a Christian as well as a police officer. Please keep my heart pure and holy and print your image on it. Keep my actions honest. Help me to realise you have put me in the community to make it a better place. May I never let you down. May my life's desire always be to pull people up and to help them no matter how they may treat me. If I ever feel badly treated help me to remember You died on the Cross to save me from all my sin. Lord, You have given me the task of law keeping. Save me from being bitter amid the unkind and cruel ways of some people when I have to watch. When sight, sound, smell or feel would bring me down please give me the courage to rise above what I see, hear, smell and touch. Above all, help me to show the community I belong to Jesus Christ. Keep on reminding me that I can do all things through Christ who gives me strength. Above all, may others see in me their hope of glory. In Jesus Name, Amen.

- APPENDIX -

SUICIDE AWARENESS

When it comes to suicide, Gary Raymond has many years of experience not only with setting out how to deal with it, but from the sheer experience of actually saving people on the brink of ending their lives. Gary well knows the heartbreak for those who are left behind to mourn the person who decided to end their life, whether impulsively or after much thought and planning.

WHAT ARE THE HIGH RISK GROUPS?
Gary lists High Risk Groups for suicide:-
- Those who have tried to suicide before
- Those who lost a significant like a spouse, parent or sibling
- Those who lost a role model such as a pop or sports star
- Those who copy a close friend's suicide (the contagion effect)
- Depressed caring professionals such as doctors, dentists, nurses, psychologists, counsellors, social workers, police officers, ambulance officers, fire fighters or rescue officers. This can include both paid and volunteer members
- The depressed, confused or mentally ill
- Victims of abuse, neglect, or bullying
- Relationships that are broken or not working
- Homosexual and gender confused people

- Those in financial trouble
- Alcohol or other substance abusers
- Those depressed due to the wrong medication
- Depressed senior citizens
- Those who fear
- Occult or cult involvement (may be multiple suicides)
- Australia's Indigenous people
- Those in police, mental health, detention or jail custody
- Young men under 25 years (high-risk group)
- People with sacrificial ideology (suicide bombers or domestic violence offenders)
- Suicide by police (those who confront police deliberately with weapons)
- Those who barricade themselves or take hostages
- Depressed terminally ill or permanently incapacitated people (euthanasia is suicide)
- Depressed defence force or former defence personnel (peacetime or combat)
- Those involved in an overwhelming critical incident or natural disaster
- Those suffering Post Traumatic Stress Disorder
- Depressed children of Vietnam veterans
- Depressed rural residents (drought then flood losses)
- Any sudden traumatic loss or change of a person or valuable thing
- Those who feel victimized after a perceived injustice, personal or emotional hurt (may make self-pity, vindictive or payback threats of suicide)

WHAT ARE THE OUTWARD SIGNS AND SYMPTOMS?

Gary asks a vital question: "What outward signs and symptoms will you first notice when looking for suicidal people?" The answer is surprising at first.

Gary says, "Usually none. A circumstance, such as a big depressing loss or change is the first suicide risk potential

SUICIDE AWARENESS

indicator. Signs and symptoms come later as their circumstances fail to resolve and people fail to cope. Chronic or acute depression in mentally ill people is an early indicator of a suicide risk as well.

"It's most important to keep an eye out for sudden unexplained improvement in a person during or after depression. It may mean they have actually decided to suicide. They develop a 'false peace' because they have finally made the decision to suicide. They have an eerie calm about it. They may say life is hopeless and they are helpless. They see their life as falling apart. Gary lists signs of those who may be a suicide risk. He advises us to be on the alert for depressed people who:

- have made previous suicide attempts
- have behaviour and personality changes
- finalise business, employment, bank, investment, and charity matters
- give away personal and valuable things
- sell sentimental or valuable things cheaply
- visit or contact relatives and friends to say goodbye
- make a will or arrange their funeral
- take out life insurance, avoid holidays, or social outings with family and friends
- become loners or get secretive
- engage in death talk or death fantasies
- joke or use 'throw off' lines about their suicide
- see a doctor without being sick to falsely obtain medication for suicide such as sleeping pills
- take time off work, truant from school or avoid education and training commitments
- obtain a gun, bring one out of storage, access military, police force or sporting weapons
- a change in normal habits
- engage in out of character sexual behaviour
- become more interested in life after death issues
- have anger outbursts or conversely, passive aggressive behaviour

- enquire about means and methods on how to die
- express unmanageable grief or trauma over a loss
- people display suicide methods or perform suicide rehearsals
- people develop eating or sleeping disorders
- behave recklessly or negligently (driving or extreme sports)
- avoid organizational commitments and neglect their team
These signs can either appear alone or in clusters

Gary passionately conveys the message the best way to find out if a person is suicidal is to ask them openly and gently as part of your normal talk with the depressed person. The best question is, "Are you suicidal?" You may ask, "'Isn't this too direct?" Yes, but directness means being open. This is what a suicidal person looks for during their struggle with suicidal thoughts and feelings. Avoidance by a carer erodes confidence in the carer's ability to relate openly to the suicidal person without fear or embarrassment.

How do you find out how deeply depressed they are? Gary says, "Ask on a scale of one to ten, where one is feeling a little down and ten is feeling devastated? This will show how they feel about themselves. The carer might misjudge them however, asking them on the scale is a 'self-assessment' by the depressed person themselves and more accurate. Later, we can use the same measurement scale to assess our progress as we give ongoing help."

Gary believes that once someone reveals they are suicidal, there are more questions to gently ask. Ask them if they have a plan. Talk about the plan. Use the how, when, where and why questions:

How are they going to suicide? (don't presume the method)
When are they going to suicide? (don't presume the time)
Where are they going to suicide? (don't presume the place)

SUICIDE AWARENESS

Why are they going to suicide? (don't presume the reason)

WHAT IS A FUTURE INVITATION?

Gary says many people are afraid that if they ask a person and they're not suicidal, that they may lose a friend. The answer is negative. People appreciate the fact you really care. If they're not suicidal at that time in their depression, give them a future invitation, just in case. Remember, believe them up front and don't call them a liar or accuse them of holding back their true feelings from you. The future invitation goes like this: "You said you're not suicidal, however if you happen to feel suicidal at any time in the future, promise you'll call me immediately. I'll get some help." The future invitation shows a deep level of care. Just explain, "I brought up the subject of suicide because I know that some depressed people get suicidal. I care enough about you to ask if it means saving your life." Gary says that asking about suicide will not give them the idea. That's a myth. Talking about suicide does not make someone suicidal.

WHY SUICIDE AWARENESS EDUCATION?

Research has proved receiving suicide awareness education and applying it reduces the incidence of suicide in the community. One of the biggest dangers in dealing with a suicidal person is to not believe them. One of the most vulnerable times for suicidal people is the time between interventions. That is after hospital stays, psychiatrist or psychologist appointments and after addiction rehabilitation programs.

WHAT IS THE SUICIDAL & HOMICIDAL RELATIONSHIP?

A big lesson for carers is to realise homicidal people may become suicidal and suicidal people may become homicidal. This becomes a safety and security issue for all involved. Psychotic mentally ill patients may become suicidal and homicidal.

WHAT ARE THE SUICIDE MYTHS?

Gary emphasizes that there are many myths when it comes to suicide. Here are some of them:-

Myth: Most suicides occur during a full moon.
False. This myth is not supported by research, however nighttime is a significant time when some depressed people are alone or under less scrutiny.

Myth: Those who suicide are mentally ill.
False. Most people who suicide have never been diagnosed with a psychiatric illness. However people with mental illness are a high risk group.

Myth: Teenagers tell their peers before their family about their suicide thoughts or plans.
True. Yes they do. Teenagers talk to other teenagers about teen problems including parents, marriage, study, career, money, drugs, sex, music, fashion and suicide.

Myth: Those who threaten suicide want attention.
False. Those who threaten suicide don't want attention. They need attention.

Myth: Those who are suicidal always tell their family.
False. Families are the least likely to be told.

Myth: Those who talk about or threaten suicide won't really do it. They are just attention seeking.
False. Talking about suicide is an indication of a serious plea for help and should be responded to immediately.

Myth: Suicide occurs without warning.
False. Eight out of ten people give warnings and display warning signs of their intent to suicide.

SUICIDE AWARENESS

Myth: Most suicidal people present indicators.
True. They communicate suicidal intentions in words, writing, actions and inactions.

Myth: It's rare for people to attempt suicide more than once.
False. Four out of five adult suicides have made previous attempts.

Myth: Mentioning suicide to a depressed person gives them the idea.
False. They already have suicidal thoughts and ideas. Mentioning it opens up honest sharing about their suicide struggle.

Myth: Suicidal people are loners.
False. Most suicidal people mix with family, workmates and community. They are ordinary people with extraordinary problems.

Myth: Suicide is genetic.
False. Research does not support this idea, however grief-driven or copycat suicides may occur after the death of a significant person in their lives. Some mental illnesses have genetic origins but not suicide itself.

Myth: If a suicidal person asks you to keep their thoughts, threats or plans a secret, you should abide by their request for confidentiality.
False. You should never keep suicide plans a secret. Tell someone who can help with the person's agreement.

Myth: Relationship breakups are common throughout your life and shouldn't cause suicidal thoughts?
False. People going through relationship breakups are a suicide risk group, especially if they were the one who didn't want the breakup to happen.

Myth: Suicidal people want to die.
False. Most suicidal people don't want to die. They just want relief from emotional pain, grief or depression.

Myth: Suicide only affects certain types of people with weak personalities.
False. Suicide affects all personality types, the young, old, rich, poor, educated, uneducated, all nationalities and religions.

Myth: Suicide is always impulsive.
False. The majority of suicides are planned. Others are impulsive and carried out in a momentary crisis, especially influenced by the person being drunk or drugged.

Myth: Self-mutilation is different from attempt suicide.
True. However, some self-mutilators may go on to complete their suicide, deliberately or accidently.

Myth: Suicide can be prevented.
True. Suicide is both detectable and preventable. More people should become 'suicide aware.' Like medical first aid, people need emotional first aid skills.

Myth: A depressing event or circumstance can be the first indicator of a suicide risk.
True. A depressing loss or change in a person's life happens before any signs of suicidal intent emerge.

Myth: We should never dare a person to commit suicide.
True. Bluffing, goading or daring someone to suicide may cause vulnerable people to do so.

Myth: To attempt suicide is a crime.

SUICIDE AWARENESS

False. It is not a criminal offence to attempt or threaten suicide. It is a criminal offence to assist someone to suicide.

Myth: Suicide notes or messages are good for relatives as they explain the reasons for the death.
False. Most suicide notes are confusing, contradictory and irrational. They may trigger grief, anger and guilt for those left behind.

Myth: Suicidal people may become aggressive.
True. Some suicidal people can be very angry and aggressive.

Myth: Suicidal people operate mainly on feelings rather than on rational thinking.
True. Most suicidal people are egocentrically (self-centered) and don't think rationally about other people when they're suicidal.

Myth: Those who joke about their suicide are not serious.
False. Those who talk about their suicide, whether in a depressive or joking manner, must be taken seriously.

Myth: We should just let some hopeless people suicide.
False. Life is a sacred gift. Suicidal people are planning a permanent solution to a temporary problem and should be encouraged to live.

Myth: Vietnam veterans' children are a high-risk suicide group.
True. In fact, the children of Vietnam veterans have three times the risk of suicide for their age group.

Myth: People never make their suicide look like an accident.
False. Some have been known to suicide on the transport system, at the workplace or at home and plan to make it look like an accident.

Myth: Once suicidal, always suicidal?
False. Many people rise from depression never again to be suicidal.

Myth: Suicide rates are higher for low-income earners.
False. Income does not discriminate in suicide.

Myth: Suicide rates are higher for women than for men.
False. Suicide attempts are higher for women, however suicide completions are higher for men.

Myth: Suicide rates are higher than homicide rates.
True. Suicide rates are much higher than homicide rates.

Myth: Victims of bullying are a suicide risk.
True. Fear and rejection cause these victims to become a suicide risk. They may also have homicidal thoughts.

WHAT IS SUICIDE CRISIS NEGOTIATION?

Stopping a suicidal person is not for the fainthearted. It takes training, skill, wisdom and patience. Negotiate is a vital word that means, 'mutual discussion and arrangement of the terms of a transaction or agreement'. Gary says when dealing with a person threatening suicide, ring the police and ambulance on 000. Focus on retrieval, not diagnosis. Focus on retrieval, not counselling, and focus on retrieval not therapy. Detailed help should be in safer place at a safer time by professionals.

HOW DO YOU PHONE CONNECT TO A SUICIIDAL PERSON?

Gary says negotiators may have to negotiate face to face, via a third person, telephone, text messaging, mail and email, internet chat rooms, two-way radio or using sign language. What should be one of the first things you say on a phone suicide crisis negotiation? Gary advises, "If we lose the connection, it's not

SUICIDE AWARENESS

me hanging up and terminating your call. Please give me your number or you ring me back if that happens". This reassures the person that if the phone connection is lost, it's not you neither hanging up on them nor neglecting their pleas for help. During or after the conversation, never hang up your phone. Use another phone to ring police on 000 for a trace or triangulation on the person's call to be initiated from the Police Communications Centre.

WHAT ARE THE WEAPON DANGERS?

When approaching someone who threatens suicide, Gary stops his approach to stay safe outside of 'kicking' or 'leg sweep' range, just in case they get aggressive. On approach there is the 'alert zone' when the person becomes aware of his presence at the scene.

The 'defence zone' is when Gary may get too close and the person gets defensive and may threaten him if he doesn't stop moving forward. Finally there's the 'attack zone' when the person may engage Gary physically with or without a weapon. Ordinary objects like nail files, combs or scissors can be turned into weapons. Whatever you do, never try to take or wrestle a weapon from a person. You may get killed or injured. Encourage them to put the weapon down and walk to you rather than you walk towards an armed person. In any case, escape and get police help. Even if you know the person, still escape. They may be homicidal.

If the person has a firearm, there is no alternative but to escape immediately, take cover and call the police. Warn others to take cover as well. Avoid approaching any person unless safe to do so. Always have an Escape Plan if things turn nasty. Gary advises:

> Work out how to escape (the method)
> When to escape (your opportunity)
> An escape queue (your excuse)
> Where to escape to (your refuge).

You may only have the opportunity to escape behind a table or into another room. If the person is dangerous to you, put space between you and them. Remember, if you escape to a room, never just lock the door. Barricade doors and windows using stacked up furniture as well. Never come out until you confirm police have arrived and have given you a direction that it's safe to.

WHAT ARE THE SAFE APPROACH & NEGOTIATION HINTS?

In your approach Gary says you should do the following:-

- Give the person audible warnings of your approach.
- Approach slowly, approach giving verbal reassurance you're there to help and not hurt them.
- Beware of environmental dangers such as loose rocks or slippery surfaces.
- Be willing to retreat and get more help if necessary.
- Plead with them assertively not to suicide and plead for time to talk and listen.
- Point out lethality (dangers) that they may be in at the present.
- Make an apology for any future errors you may make in your speech or actions toward them, just in case. This assures them that if you make mistakes, they are not intentional.
- Ask compliance questions such as, "What do I have to do, or not do, to prevent your suicide"?
- Clear the scene of people who threaten the safety or security of successful negotiations.
- Quarantine the scene from uninvited intrusions on the negotiation by forming perimeters creating an exclusion zone.
- Beware of the person's suicide exhibition behaviour, which is the deliberate acting out of the first stages of the suicidal method, like leaning out over the edge, swinging out over the edge or letting go of handholds.

SUICIDE AWARENESS

- Caution, the exhibition behaviour may be a suicide rehearsal.
- Be assertive and gently directive.
- Discourage exhibition behaviour as they may 'accidentally' fall over the edge.
- Assure them you believe their threat.
- Point out the dangers to them.
- Point out they may "slip and fall"
- Plead with them to keep still.
- In your speech, don't be submissive but be assertive and not aggressive.

Gary points out that during a negotiation try not to say *If*, but *When*. "*When* you come back from the edge we will help you with counselling". When is positive and shows you really believe they will not die and there is hope.

Also during a negotiation try not to say *I*, but rather *We*. "When you come back from the edge we will help you receive helpful counselling". This shows that many people are ready to help. It's being a team.

HOW LETHAL IS THE THREAT?
"Negotiators need to assess how deadly the threat really is," Gary says.
- What is suicidal person's intent?
- What is the suicide location like?
- What is the suicide method or means?
- Are they threatening suicide verbally, physically or both?
- Are they unable to control their emotions/actions?
- Are they staring into space or not communicating?
- Are they constantly staring at the suicide means?
- Are they hiding or running away from help?

When dealing with suicidal people:
- Notify someone or take someone along with you and arrange regular updates of your progress

- Seek advice until police and ambulance arrive.
- Ensure you have referral details to professional help if required.

HOW DOES THE NEGOTIATOR RESPOND?
Beware of the person's anger. Take them seriously. Don't joke or laugh at their jokes. Do not 'mirror' their behaviour or use bad language. Encourage them to talk out their homicidal ideation. They may be thinking of killing someone they perceive as causing the situation they are in. It helps them to vent, distracts from the suicide threat and buys you time. Look for evidence of barricading/hostage taking by the person, violence against other people or pets, violence against property, alternative suicide/homicide means, evidence of 'concealment' (hiding something or someone), and watch their access to a motor vehicle.

WHAT IS PERTURBATION?
Gary cleverly explains perturbation. He says that perturbation refers to how upset the suicidal person is. It's like a thermometer, the person's emotional temperature. Often in their mind, they're confused or calculating decisions. It's a pendulum of life and death. They are indecisive at this time. "Will I or won't I suicide"? It's the suicide struggle not the depressive losses or changes that are the issue in the present tense that the person is going through. They put their problems aside and just concentrate on whether to suicide or not. The carer should make the suicidal person aware that they know about the struggle in their mind that is occurring and invite the person to discuss it openly. We also negotiate the retreat of actions one step at a time (de-staging.).

Unfortunately, once the person has decided to suicide, they then have a cognitive (mind) struggle as to when to suicide. Right time or wrong time to suicide is the new issue. Ascertain the significance of the timing, if any. It may be an anniversary or other significant date or time for the person. You may have to intensify the negotiation if a deadline has been set by the person.

SUICIDE AWARENESS

They may tell you when they're going to do it. Plead for more time.

WHEN CAN BE A CRITICAL TIME?
Sunset & sunrise can be critical a time for some suicidal people, says Gary. Some suicidal people protest, "I just can't face another day". Or conversely, "I just can't face another night". Ascertain if they hate or fear the day or the night. Attempt to retrieve the person before their vulnerable time. Promise help and supervision for their vulnerable time. Attempt to persuade them the timing is wrong and not suicide at this time. Beware of sudden unexplained improvement during a suicide crisis. It may mean a decision to suicide has been made.

Gary says, "It's vital to try and stay in the present tense when negotiating with a suicidal person. Their present circumstance is the most dangerous. The present is changeable but the past is unchangeable, with the future unknown. Allow them to talk about the past and future, however keep steering them gently back to the present contract and retrieval plan. Explore their present tense cognitive (thoughts), present tense emotional, present tense physical, present tense behavioural and present tense spiritual.

"Caution with sedation or medication in the field. The suicidal person may already have substances in their body. Prohibit the taking of medication or alcohol during a suicide negotiation, as the outcome is too unpredictable and may cause an altered level of consciousness or behaviour of the person. They should be medicated at a safer time and place under medical supervision. Ambulance transport and medical supervision is vital, not in the rear of a police vehicle in this case. Use only as much force as necessary. Ensure prevention of injury and caution with their breathing 'mechanics' during restraint. Ask for mental health team or paramedic ambulance transport with police escort.

"When assessing a suicidal person, watch their facial expressions, listen for vocal clues such s the content and manner of their speech. Watch the person's breathing rate. Not so much for physical reasons, but to monitor emotional changes and measure perturbation. Their posture, gestures and actions will give you clues. Clothing and grooming (wrong clothes for the weather conditions), injuries or illness could mean a previous suicide attempt, previous self-mutilation or self-abuse, victim of violence, injured whilst on drugs and/or alcohol. The suicidal person could even be an offender threatening suicide after committing a criminal act, which may be a dangerous situation for the carer. The person may run away and hide, may run away to a more dangerous location or they may run away to locate a weapon and may return. Reassure the suicidal person they are not in trouble with the police for their suicide threats or attempts.

"Explain that they will still be taken to a 'help' facility by the police or ambulance. In most cases, negotiating time decreases perturbation. The longer you can engage a suicidal person in dialogue, the better chance of successful retrieval to professional help. This may also give them time to 'sober up'. In other cases the longer the time the more critical the situation becomes as perturbation and lethality may even rise. All negotiations are unique in character. Encourage them to think and talk in 'retrieval time'. Remember 'when' not 'if'. If you have to, plead for more time, do it. Discuss the contracts you have made with them, ask them for detail or repeats of what's on their mind. Ask them clarifying questions without 'cross examining' them. Use physical needs such as a blanket or drink of water (only with medical permission) to get them back. Use location difficulties such as extreme winds, heat, lightening, rain, cold or darkness to convince them to come back."

HOW DO WE DEAL WITH DEMANDS & REQUESTS?

Gary insists the negotiator should not normally initiate demands or offers to the suicidal person. Why? The demands or offers may be unrealistic, unwanted, inappropriate or even harmful. In most cases wait for the suicidal person to make demands or offers. It may come in the form of:

SUICIDE AWARENESS

A direct request: "May I have cigarette?"
An indirect request: "I would feel better if I had a cigarette"
A bargain: "I promise I'll not suicide if you give me a cigarette"
A threat: "If you don't give me a cigarette I'll suicide"
A plea: "Oh please, please give me cigarette"

Evaluate each request on its merit. Never say "no" to demands, say "yes", but introduce lots and lots of difficulties with meeting the demand. Involve the suicidal person in solving their own demands. Use the demands to 'buy' time and validate their trust in your ability to help. Remember, give honest and factual evidence of your commitment to progress their demand.

HOW DO WE PREVENT INTERFERENCE DURING THE NEGOTIATION?

Gary was very stern when he explained the following. Don't allow spouses, relatives, friends or workmates to negotiate with a person threatening suicide. They usually exaggerate or trivialize the issues raised. These people may become aroused emotionally and threaten, insult, ridicule or dump guilt and shame on the suicidal person. This will be a negative impact to the success of a safe retrieval. It will also arouse the suicidal person. Anger, frustration, fear, yelling and arguments between them may result. On some occasions, people have been known to complete their suicide after such upsetting encounters. Tell the suicidal person that contact with these people may be made with professional supervision after their retrieval.

WHAT IS MEANT BY THE FACTS & FEELINGS?

Gary also uses the 'FF' Principle. That is Facts and Feelings. Acknowledge the suicidal person's facts and feelings in the conversation. They may say, "I'm upset because my wife left me." The fact is their wife left; the feeling is they're upset. Let the person know you heard the fact and the way they feel about it as well. If the negotiator just acknowledges facts, the person's feelings will be missed or ignored. Conversely, if the feelings are overemphasized, important facts are missed. Remember, people want to be listened too.

WHAT ARE SOME OF THE DANGERS?
Gary wisely advises not to engage in emotional or factual probing of a suicidal person, especially victims of crime or abuse. It's too traumatic during suicide crisis negotiation to bring up their trauma event and may even raise their emotional arousal to a dangerous level. Save any emotional or factual probing or other in-depth therapy for controlled and safer counselling conditions by professionals. Remember, safer place and safer time.

Watch for:
- weapons
- projectiles or hazardous materials
- 'booby traps'
- improvised explosive devices (IED), chemical or incendiary bombs
- 'home made suicide apparatus' (such as electric chairs, firearm racks)

We can't presume that all weapons or devices are for self-harm only. They could be used to harm you or others as well. The suicidal person may carry more than one weapon or device. An extensive search of the person and their surrounding location, by police, is required on retrieval of the suicidal person.

WHAT IS THE 'ACTIVE TALKING' MODEL?
When the suicidal person indicates they are just about to do it, urgently use the negotiation 'Active Talking Model' not the 'Active Listening Model' Active talking is compassionate and direct with caring authority and assertiveness. Gary says, "It's a strong and urgent plea for someone's life. Tell the person not to suicide. Give them directions to reverse their actions back

to a stable condition. Tell them you care and to give the future a go. When a person is retrieved, ensure they are kept under supervision until professional help is obtained."

WHO CARES FOR THE CARER?
Gary explains, "Whether you negotiated a suicide crisis successfully or unsuccessfully, ensure you consider defusing or debriefing with a support person or support group to make sure you're okay. In other words, he says, "Who cares for the carer"?

"I'm never down, just up or getting up"
John C. Maxwell

"Come to Me all who are weary and heavy laden and I will give you rest."
Jesus. The Bible, Matthew 11:28.

For support contact The Salvation Army's Suicide Prevention and Bereavement website:-
www.suicideprevention.salvos.org.au

Contact Gary on garyraym@ozemail.com.au

ABOUT THE AUTHOR
- DAVID R NICHOLAS -

David Nicholas is a Baptist pastor who was born in Bristol, England. David has been published in many newspapers and magazines in Australia, England and the United States where he lived with his family for five years while he obtained a Master's degree in Journalism and a Master of Science in Radio and Television. *Harper Collins* published David's book of Australian stories *Musical Wheat* in 1997.

David was responsible for the creation of The Millthorpe District Museum. He was also the driving force behind a latch key project—the development of a private school (Inaburra) at Menai, south of Sydney. David has also ministered to churches in America, New South Wales, South Australia and Tasmania. He is married to Judith. They have 3 children Mark, Joanne and Andrew.

OTHER BOOKS BY - DAVID R NICHOLAS -

The Pacemaker	*Musical Wheat*
Honeymoon Corner	*Journeys With God*
Wigs	*Changing Tides*
Decurio (In Process)	*Dingo Treasure (in process)*
Top Cop (Book One)	

For more information or to order please contact David Nicholas via email ronald.31@bigpond.com

www.ingramcontent.com/pod-product-compliance
Lightning Source LLC
LaVergne TN
LVHW051517070426
835507LV00023B/3163